Conjuring Black Funk

To Zinzi,

Thank you for your
spirit + love.

May you enjoy
peace, pleasure, +
passion always

AC

Conjuring Black Funk:

Notes on Culture, Sexuality, and Spirituality,

Volume I

Herukhuti

VINTAGE
ENTITY
PRESS

2007

Conjuring Black Funk: Notes on Culture, Sexuality, and Spirituality, Volume 1

Copyright © 2007 by Herukhuti (Hameed Williams)

Published by:

Vintage Entity Press
P.O. Box 211
New York, New York 10037

07 08 09 10 11 10 9 8 7 6 5 4 3 2 1

Second Printing
Cover art copyright © 2007 by Charly Dominguez
Cover design by DeShon Gales for Flatfoot Designs
Layout by Michael-Christopher
Printed in the United States of America

Library of Congress Control Number:

ISBN 0-9752987-3-9
ISBN 13: 978-0-9752987-3-2

$15.95

At the heart of every revolutionary effort is the question of how I can transform myself as I work to transform society. – Amiri Baraka

Dedication

To all my teachers and all my students,
To all my mentors and all my mentees, and
To all my parents and all my progeny,
This book is dedicated to you and what you have
inspired within me.

Acknowledgements

Thank you to:
My spirit guides and ancestors;
Members of The Brotherhood of African Men & The Sisterhood of
African Women;
The L.A. Family;
My NYC men's group;
The Harlem Training Group for Diasporic Africans in Dagara
Medicine;
All the participants of Our Bodies, Our Wisdom, The Model for Life,
Sensual Yoga, & Erotic Play for Men;
Adodi International;
My friends & colleagues in the academy;
Vintage Entity Press staff, friends, & allies;
All my lovers, fuck buddies, & one-night stands;
My Queer Family;
My genealogical/genetic family;
And all those theorists/scholars, activists, conjurers, & cultural
animators who have inspired, excited, and challenged me to do better
with my craft.

Thank you to Samuel R. Delany (foreword author), Charly Joaquin
Dominguez (cover art), Steven G. Fullwood (editor/publisher),
DeShon Gales (cover design), Carla Robinson (manuscript proofreader),
Michael-Christopher (manuscript layout), and Charles F. Stephens
(original co-conceiver) for their contributions in the birthing of
this book.

TABLE OF CONTENTS

Foreword

Thinkers can often be judged by what they love. Herukhuti writes: "There are three things that I love: spirituality, Black folks, and sex." These are dangerous things for a Black man to love. To love them—to state your love for them—is to risk being dismissed as another eccentric sex-mad Black mystic. But what goes down here makes too much sense to dismiss. There is much intelligence here, on topics from relationships to the sexual bravery of coming out. If you are scared to come out of any sexual closet, this book may encourage you to do so in community with others. What a difference the support of a community makes—something that Herukhuti knows and writes about incisively and beautifully.

This is a book we need to read—all of us.

This is a book we need to think about—all of us.

This is a book we need to know—all of us.

In his own introduction, Herukhuti writes that this is a book that he wants us to read *now*. It's a book that has grown out of his more recent observations of the world, the events of the times, and what can be observed around us. But paradoxically, I can't think of a time in the past forty years when this would not have been a salutary read for the vast majority of folks I know, not only those of us who are black and/or spiritual, but for pretty much everyone I know interested in a rewarding life. Nor would I be surprised if it were just as useful forty years from now. Its timelessness grows, if anything, *from* its specificity.

The intelligence in this book pours out in wonderful, small nuggets. It's warming to see Audre Lorde's bitter obiter dictum "the master's tools cannot be used to dismantle the master's house" made to reverse itself and grow up, in "How We Use the Master's Tools to Dismantle Our Own House." It's literally wonderful to read Herukhuti on body fascism in the gay community. This is truly adventurous stuff. And Herukhuti ends the first part of his collection with a beautiful piece of intelligence that I hope everyone can internalize:

> I will [take] this moment to say, with the same feeling of naturalness, privilege, and entitlement that people who identify as straight or heterosexual would, "I loving fucking without condoms and do so every opportunity that I can." Now ask me how I do it and you might learn something.

It's the closing sentence, of course, that embodies the smarts.

The node of Herukhuti's philosophy is that we are conceived from moments of sexual passion. Thus it behooves us not to lose sight of our origins. Herukhuti moves from there through a cold, harsh look at what the "must" of monogamy reflects of our faithless society, and onto another cascade of commonsensical intelligence about the reality of polyamory. Since this is the way I've managed to live my own life, and since I know many others who have as well, again it's wonderful to see Herukhuti proclaiming that all relationships are hard work, and require honesty, compassion, and concern for the feelings of the other(s) involved.

Looking for something to disagree with among these pages for me is an exercise in scraping the bottom of the barrel. But I do take issue with one aspect of the work. At one point Herukhuti gives some tips on when he feels it's time to end a relationship with a lover. I might have agreed with him a hundred percent when I was twenty-five—then I shamefully kept some relationships going in spite of the fact that they violated one or another strictures on his list. But now, at sixty-five, I find myself wondering if he hasn't set the bar a little too high; which is to say before you end things, it doesn't hurt to think seriously about what you're getting in return and asking if it's worth it or, indeed, about the emotionally, sexually, and psychologically purpose of a given relationship. If your lover likes to be told what a big dick he has—it makes him smile a lot, turns him on, and generally feel good for a couple of hours (and nobody else ever mentions it to him outside the relationship, where, actually, it rather embarrasses him), it seems somewhat draconian to withhold this—especially if you enjoy it, too— just because it's emotionally "immature." The point is that all pleasure begins as fundamentally childish—immature in the *most* fundamental and basic way.

On the other hand, at least once in my life I have told a lover, "If you *ever* hit me again, this relationship is over!" And, seven years later, when he punched me in the jaw and broke my glasses, I stuck to my guns. He was out that night.

So read the words that come after this note carefully and with attention.

You will be better for it.

Now enjoy.

—Samuel R. Delany

Introduction

Conjuring: (n) The process or product of making
magic; a gathering of folks with the purpose of doing a
"work;" a sexual or erotic experience that is ritualistic
and pregnant with intimacy, passion, and desire; the
work of bush doctors, hoodoo folks, conjure women,
shamans, blues artists, jazz musicians, funk masters,
tribal house magicians, underground hip hop heads,
practitioners of the arts and sciences of the black
hand, the underbelly and crossroads, as well as the
followers of the Black Mama, the Lady with the Thick
Thighs, and She Who Dances in Blood and Fire.

(v) The present progressive tense of the verb conjure;
to use desire, intentionality, and spiritual power to
mix elements from the environment in a manner that
produces a magical effect; to work roots; to trouble the
waters; to call into physical reality that which is germi-
nated in the loins, believed in the heart, and conceived
in the mind.

Though you may not have come to realize it yet, I wrote this book
specifically for you. For the time that you read it, you and I—as well as all
those who have walked with me through my life, and all those who have
walked with you through your life—will be in a series of conversations
about culture, sexuality, and spirituality. This introduction and the
pages that follow have multiple purposes—theoretical text and a book
of conjuring.

As a theoretical text, the book is a way for me to document my
journeys so that other seekers on The Path That Is Not Obvious can
observe and learn from my experiences and revelations. In that sense,
this book is a treatise, if you will. It documents and articulates a way of
framing the multiple realities that I have experienced. It structures my
perceptions into—what I hope is—an emerging/emergent theoretical
framework, that I call, Afrocentric Decolonizing Queer Theory
(ADQT).

The history of "theory" and people of color, particularly Black
folks, is a complex one. Barbara Christian once said that Black folks do

theorizing, rather than theory. We conjure theories like we have conjured so much that has kept us, through colonization, slavery, apartheid, and neo-colonialism—we make something out of almost nothing. Theory for us is an active process of creation, re-creation, renewal, and healing. Bell hooks, in sharing her experiences with theory, said that she came to theory for healing. It was a balm that soothed her as she dealt with the impact of living Black and female in a white supremacist, sexist, and heterosexist society.

ADQT is theorizing rather than a theory. Its foundations are Black Feminist Thought, Black/Postcolonial Queer Theory, and Afrocentricity. Black Feminist Thought provides the tools for analyzing the moments when race, gender, and class intersect. Through Audre Lorde, it locates liberatory struggle in the use of the erotic as a power. Black/Postcolonial Queer Theory articulates the politics of transgression as resistance, self-affirmation, and the suggestion of alternatives to erotophobia. Ibrahim Abdurrahman Farajaje's articulation of the primacy of embodiment in our liberation is instructive in that regard. Samuel R. Delany's explorations of the borderlands of sexual, cultural, racial, and gendered social space are also important contributions. Afrocentricity is the cultural landscape upon which ADQT grows. In the context of ADQT, Afrocentricity is the spiritual-cultural-ontological-epistemological-axiological link that continental, Diasporic, and Kiasporic Africans establish with our African heritage. It is a critical Afrocentricity that challenges the heterosexism, erotophohia, hegemonic masculinity, sexism, classism, and inflexibility of other forms of Afrocentric thought.

Because this book is an expression of ADQT, each piece is a demonstration of its use as a challenge to the psychic and cultural bondage of life in 21st Century United States. In addition to creating a challenge, the pieces also offer hope for something different; in fact, there is much hope for a host of somethings that are different. My hope is that, as you read this work, you find within your being any place from which hitherto for you have been estranged. We are at our most powerful when we are fully embodied, being not divorced from any aspect of ourselves no matter how socially discouraged.

This book is also a conjuring book. It was created with the intention that you would use it as a tool to conjure queer realities, transgressive moments, and liberatory experiences. Within each piece, there are ingredients for social hoodoo spells that when used appropriately can tear at the dominant social order and give birth to a socially and ecologically just world. Like the mystical books of Kemet-Kush (ancient Egyptian-Nubia), the book will bear its magic to your level of comprehension. *To those with the eyes to see, the truth of the wor(l)d is revealed.*

As a conjuring book, the text is alive and brought to life through your reading. The time, place, context, and purpose of your reading will affect what is produced as you read. So think about how you want to read this book. Reading the book alone will be different than reading it with others. Reading the book for a class will be different than reading the book for personal interest. Reading the book in the nude will be different than reading the book clothed. Reading the book while you feel aroused will be different than reading the book when you're feeling grief. We can conjure many things with the appropriate intentionality. Therefore, I advise you to be intentional with your reading of this work.

Books of magic are never just the products of their authors. This book is no exception. Though I am its author, *Conjuring Black Funk* is a product of various conjurers, juju folk, seducers, and practitioners of the erotic arts. My life with these folks has produced a knowledge that I am sharing with you in the form of these notes. But don't mistake the symbol for the thing itself. Although I have attempted to render a body of work that is useful and alive, it is still a collection that has no flesh and therefore lacks the texture, taste, and smell that can only come from connecting with the embodied knowledge that pulsates within me.

Your life, therefore, adds the flesh to the word as you take up these spells and use them to conjure. Through your engagement of the world and your reading of these words, you call your visceral, spiritual, emotional, and social selves to reform and refashion the embodied knowledge that was a part of the genesis of this work. In that way, we are conjuring together, intertwining certain aspects of ourselves in acts of tantric magic and social transformation. Conjuring together brings us to become the change we want to see in the world.

To conjure, one takes on a set of responsibilities. When, in the act of conjuring, you connect to a previously hidden truth, you are responsible for incorporating that truth into your being, placing it in its proper position, and using it when the time is right. To ignore a truth that has emerged through a conjuring betrays the act of conjuring itself and damages our relationship to the work. Don't turn your back on anything that is revealed to you through these pages. Learn to live with the truths.

We are also responsible, in our conjuring, to be clear, purposeful, and ethical. As you work with this book, make sure to use it with clarity, purpose, and ethics. Conjuring can be a shield or a weapon, something that builds or something that tears down, something that births or something that calls death into being. Be clear about why you use this work and the potential consequences of your actions.

Though many of elements of the book appear as essays, they are just as magical as any spell written in a traditional form. Part of the magic rests in how you are affected by the text. Another part of the magic is in how you affect the world based upon your engagement of the text. Divided into three sections—culture, sexuality, and spirituality—the book highlights selected thoughts, actions, and experiences from 1997-2007. During that period, I practiced a polyamorous, bisexual relationship with a woman for five years; obtained a PhD; co-parented two children into adolescence; completed an HIV research assistantship at one of the nation's foremost research centers for the clinical and behavioral study of HIV; built a sexual cultural center for people of color called Black Funk; performed ritual, sexual alchemy, and Bondage Domination/Submission Sadomasochism (BDSM) sex with numerous individuals; started a queer family; trained in Dagara shamanism; wrote this book; and provided counseling to various individuals as a priest/shaman, life coach, and sexologist. There are minimal references, in the scholarly form, used. Instead, I have provided a bibliography at the end of the book for you to seek out other texts that have informed this one. The magic of each of the elements of the book is taken from the essence of those experiences. I am honored to share the magic and theorizing of those experiences with you in the pages that follow.

Culture

WHAT THE FUNK...WHY THE FUNK...HOW THE FUNK?

In 2002, Black Funk was born. Like all births, there was much that preceded it that informed what emerged at the time of birth. Prior to 2002, I had been offering workshops (e.g., Communication for Couples, Model for Life, Erotic Play for Men), teaching classes (e.g., Sensual Yoga), hosting sex parties (e.g., The Workshop), and sharing knowledge of the erotic arts and sensual sciences (e.g. Tantra and Kundalini Yoga, massage, and Tai Chi Chuan/Chi Qong). Through those experiences, I met a lot of great people. Over time, it became clear that a great need existed within people of color communities affected by Western/

European colonization and cultural hegemony for empowerment that included a space for sexual healing and sensual liberation. The idea of a sexual cultural center emerged as a way to address the need that I perceived. Black Funk became that center.

People frequently ask me why I have created Black Funk. Within their questioning, they hope to understand the means by which I am able to approach as normal, everyday and casual even, the expression of sexuality and sensuality by people of color. For them, the "how" is an important way to map my journey to work in an area of human development with an approach to that area that many find provocative, oppositional, controversial, iconoclastic, confrontational, transgressive, profane, and obscene. There are certain topics that we don't discuss in polite conversation, in public discourse, or in the myriad of simultaneous monologues that we call the "academic community" or the "cultural community."

When we invert the questions of "why" and "how," there are penetrating (see the dick) and enveloping (see the pussy) truths waiting there—why/how did Black Funk create me? Black Funk created me through the preparation of my soul gestating in the black primordial waters of the Great Mother. Black Funk stirred the lust, love, passion, and cravings of my mother and father to desire each other, to want to taste each other's sun-baked flesh. My mother wanted to feel my father's firmed phallus seeking a home in her—if only for a moment. My father wanted to experience the deep guttural satisfaction of my mother's warm wet yoni surrounding his erection with the rhythms of her womb. Their sex was Black Funk. Their sex, Black Funk, provided the conduit through which my soul re-entered this world to produce my life's purpose.

I was born of passion. Think about that for a second in relation to how you came into this life. Many of us are born in/of/because of passion. That passion, that Black Funk, courses through our blood vessels. It heats our blood, warms our hearts, and stirs our souls. Black Funk is the germinating force of existence.

There has been no more appropriate time in human history to acknowledge the power and presence of Black Funk. There are reactionary forces at work to de-Funk the world. Those forces use the military power of government and commerce as well as the dogmatic power of religion to de-Funk the world. While HIV/AIDS—one of the greatest threats to the full enjoyment of sex and intimacy—has raged across the globe endangering the lives and loving of EVERYONE regardless of sexual identity, we have had:

- A US president remove a Black woman from the position of the nation's chief medical officer because she dared to suggest that we teach young people how to manage their natural sexual urges through the practice of masturbation,
- Two other US presidents who have made medical professionals in the non-European world choose between having the funds to adequately address the medical needs of their patients and providing their patients with a comprehensive set of reproductive options,
- Pharmaceutical companies that have exploited the consequences of neo-colonialism in their pricing and distribution of HIV medications,
- Decision-makers and personalities in the media (news and entertainment) who have used scapegoating, sensationalism, and fabrication to pit us against each other under the guise of providing public health information and identifying the risk factors in HIV transmission,
- So-called community leaders who have turned a blind eye and a deaf ear, hardened their hearts to the very real, very human factors associated with negotiating one's natural desires for sexual/sensual pleasure and human connection in an environment in which greater risks are associated with doing so than ever before.

I believe that the healing, liberating, and rejuvenating resources we need for the planet and ourselves are restored within Black Funk. So I return to the funk, the Black Funk, in an effort to reclaim, affirm, and resurrect my birthright—to live, to love, and to learn.

Are you ready to walk into Black Funk with me?

WHY ARE YOU A SEXOLOGIST?
AN INTERVIEW BY
STEVEN G. FULLWOOD

Ok, so what is a sexologist?

A sexologist is someone who is obsessed with sex and is smart enough to find ways of normalizing, validating, professionalizing, and commodifing his/her obsession. Sexologists find ways of making "scientific" their passion for sex. We are open to systematically exploring any question, concept, or problem related to sex and sexuality. Frequently sexologists have been trained in various disciplines including sociology, anthropology, medicine, and psychology before focusing on sexology as a discipline. They then receive additional training or experience specific to sexology.

Sexologists are different from sex therapists although someone can be both. While a sexologist is oftentimes interested in studying sex and sexuality, a sex therapist is oftentimes interested in treating what Western science deems "sexual dysfunctions"—not being able to get your dick hard or your pussy wet or letting loose the juice too early or having fantasies, engaging in behaviors, experiencing feelings related to sex that impair your ability to accomplish other goals in your life.

I am a sexologist and a sex educator. One day I want to achieve certification as a sex therapist. Currently there is only one state in the US that has professionalized recognition of sex therapy - Florida. That must be because of Luther Campbell/2 Live Crew and all the Cubans, Haitians, and retired European Jews that are concentrated in Florida. But seriously, I don't know why Florida and not other states.

There are a few professional organizations for sexologists. The most notable is the Society for the Scientific Study of Sexuality (SSSS). There are a few professional organizations for sex therapists and sex educators. The most notable are the American Association of Sex Educators, Counselors, and Therapists (AASECT) and the Sexuality Information and Education Council of the United States (SIECUS).

Why did you decide to become a sexologist?

There are three things that I love: spirituality, Black folks, and sex. When I considered entering a doctoral program, I also considered how I could combine those three loves in an academic and professional context. Fortunately, I found a non-traditional, interdisciplinary PhD program that allowed me the flexibility to accomplish that task.

Since I was a kid I was deeply interested in the liberation struggles of African Diasporic people. As I grew up, my analysis revealed a dearth of exploration into the intersection of our spirituality, our sexuality, and our culture by the social activists and social theorists I studied. A few years ago, I made a commitment to working in that area—the intersection of our spirituality, our sexuality, and our culture.

Do you and other sexologists get together every now and then and discuss your work?

Yes. SSSS has a national conference every year as well as a West Coast regional conference and a Midwest/East Coast regional conference. In NY, the HIV Center for Clinical and Behavioral Studies hosts weekly symposia on Thursdays, 9:30am-11:00am.

I like saying the word "sexologist." Can you tell?

Yes, but that's quite predictable. Sexologists have proved that having a sexologist in your mouth causes your brain to receive signals from the nerves in your mouth and throat that the brain registers as pleasurable. There are also medicinal properties associated with having a sexologist in your mouth.

What's the worst part of your job as a sexologist? Please explain.
Telling people they can't have sex with me.

Describe the purpose and function of Black Funk.
Black Funk is a sexual cultural center for people of color of various sexual orientations, desires, pleasures, interests, and passions. I founded it with the help of a few friends and supporters. We are growing into a place for people of color to share, research, and explore sexual education, sexual information, erotic aesthetics, and sexual culture from a sex positive, body positive, Afrocentric perspective.

We have an online discussion forum that people of color can join to get more information and to engage in conversation on sexuality related issues. You can find out more about Black Funk by coming to our site, http://www.blackfunk.org.

In what ways do Black people need to heal? How can these things be accomplished?
Black People don't need to heal. We can choose to heal or choose not to heal. The universe will do what it needs to do to survive. There are places and spaces within our collective body in which healing, from my perspective, would be appropriate. We have yet, in any kind of collective and or systematic way, to assess the impact of chattel slavery and colonialism on our physiosexual (our physical), psychosexual (our emotional), sociosexual (our social), and metaphysiosexual (our spiritual) persons. Having not made those assessments, we have yet to uncover all the ways we have been wounded and all the ways in which healing may be appropriate.

I am biased in this regard but I think we need more people committed to a critical and vigorous use of Afrocentric thought to explore these areas, uncover these stories, and maintain our access to these worlds.

September 13, 2003

PORN, PLEASURE, AND PROFIT

My perspective on the topic of pornography is informed by my experience in the adult entertainment and sex industry as a businessperson and a consumer. As a consumer, I have often been critical of Black (gay) porn videos for a lack of originality, authenticity, intimacy, and real engagement in their portrayal of human relations. But what has given me pause in my eagerness to make those criticisms is the acknowledgment that I have continued to consume/view porn despite my criticisms. Despite my critique, I still engage in the behavior that the producers of porn want—consumption. Admittedly, I don't buy porn. I access free porn sources. I think porn pricing is artificially high because of government regulation and social marginalization. There's no reason why a new video of porn should cost more than a new video of any other kind of movie. The only reason why it does is because the value of porn is inflated by the marginalized status of pornography. Despite the outcries some in the industry make in arguing against government infringement of their first amendment rights, porn producers are making a financial killing because government artificially limits their products.

Porn producers have little motivation to create the kind of porn that people—mainly, but not exclusively, female—often say they want: porn that is a closer representation of reality, porn that portrays more intimacy and connectedness between the performers. That's because people—mainly, but not exclusively, male—continue to buy what currently exists. Experimenting with the formula in any significant way could mean a loss of money and loss of brand loyalty among customers. When Blatino gay porn director, Enrique Cruz of LaMancha Videos and Enrique Cruz Presents, took the porn genre of the "extended hip hop video" and developed it into his own style of porn, he was taking a risk, yes, but it was a risk that was based upon the success of a formula that had already existed and was consistent with the pop culture themes of the time. Black Male Wrestling (BMW) has done something similar with its wrestling videos. But there are many ways in which both producers stay comfortably within the boundaries of stereotypes, clichés, social expectations, and formulas. They do so because we, the majority of us, have proved over time that we will purchase it.

So for example, a man with a six pack or 8+ dick or slim-toned body, or a woman with a fat ass, big titties, and thick lips, will be more often than not the focus of our consumer activity in pursuit of sexual entertainment than a brother with a gut, a less than 8-inch dick, or a woman with a belly and small, drooping titties. We may purchase and watch the latter once or twice but the former brings the most money. What's more saddening to me is those of us who don't look like the gym-bodied man or woman but who want to see him/her fuck rather than someone who looks more like us. Porn actor and producer Ty Lattimore of Ty Lattimore Entertainment has, over the last years, attempted to change that reality. He has produced videos with performers who are not conventionally attractive in a pop culture sense. Ty's body—featured in most of his company's videos—has evolved over the years, incorporating a protruding belly. Ty has definitely attempted to take chances in casting and content as he, almost single-handedly, expands the genre of black gay porn produced by Black people.

Another reality of the porn industry is the dearth of people who are in the industry because they are sexually liberated and empowered individuals who have a healthy sense of sexual play and a desire to express their sexuality while being compensated for that expression as compared to the number of people in the industry who are trying to make some cash out of economic desperation. With the former you might get performances that are inspired and inspiring. You might get sexual and theatrical creativity that makes you cum every time. With the latter, you are likely to get the bare minimum that will get you off, hopefully. Few porn actors are trained actors. They may meet each other just 10 minutes before shooting. As individuals, they are not necessarily great lovers. Porn actors are chosen for their look. They keep getting work because of their look. Their performance is a secondary concern. Therefore, our expectations of them—to be creative, sensual, sexually experimental, and hot all while fucking in front of a production crew and with the knowledge that thousands of people are going to be scrutinizing every inch of their body and their performance—are quite high, considering.

If you have been on the set of a movie, you will recognize how much of the artificiality of the final product is caused by the technical demands at play. Think about the complexity of sexual performance. How does one capture all of the various angles, points of contact, exchanges, etc. that happen between two or more bodies in a way that doesn't obstruct your viewing, distract/disturb the actors, or miss some other important shot? And how many of the directors, camera operators, lighting people, and scriptwriters are trained for or possess professional experience in the area of work they perform in porn?

I think that both porn professionals and porn consumers share responsibility for the state of porn today. When I read/listen to the personal ads or hook-up messages online and on the phone lines, I read/hear people request the exact same images, scenarios, and themes that are portrayed in porno. That tells me there's an interdependent flow of influence between porn producers and consumers, both influencing each other.

The same can be said for sex events. People bemoan the physical-type restrictions, the gender restrictions, sexual identity, or some other restrictions (couples only) that are enforced by proprietors of sex parties, sex spaces, and other erotic events. But proprietors are trying to conform to the needs of the market—the market meaning the largest number of people who are most likely to patronize them. Those are the realities of the marketplace. If you don't like what's available, take into consideration the degree of marginality your particular desire has in the marketplace. Consider whether you would be willing to invest your life savings in a business that offered what you are seeking. If the answer is no, then your next step isn't to try to get the current businesses to offer it. Your next step is to turn other people on to the interest you have. You have to engage in grassroots organizing in your own bedroom to change the culture. When enough people are into the fetish or desire you have, businesses will respond to serve that market. That's consumer empowerment/responsibility.

We build institutions with our labor and our sweat. If you're not actively and consistently supporting products, services, and businesses (e.g., with cash, purchasing, and/or patronage) that you feel offer something different, then you have no right to complain about the bullshit that's out there.

HOGG BY SAMUEL R. DELANY
- A REVIEW

Samuel R. Delany wrote *Hogg* in 1969. It wasn't until 1995 that the novel was first published. It wasn't published again until 2004. Why, you ask, did a work by an author of such an immense following and acclaimed writing career as Delany have such a difficult time getting to press and getting into the hands of readers? Because the story is filled with pedophilia, the rape and abuse of women and children, homosexual sex, interracial racialized sex, piss drinking, cum swallowing, shit eating, sadistic brutality, and condomless sex. The word "nigger" and its derivative "Nigg" are probably used more times than in a Richard Pryor comedy album. *Hogg* is offensive, disturbing, corrupting, and

27

nauseating.

The narrator of the story is a young boy, 10 years old, who is homeless. He gets pimped out by another kid, along with the kid's sister, to whomever in the neighborhood that will pay 25 cents to fuck his mouth and ass. These patrons include members of a biker club and some "niggers."

Later, he hooks up with a man named Hogg, who is hired to execute vengeance against women who have wronged his clients. The vengeance is carried out brutally with each woman being beaten, to a point at which any human being would piss and/or shit on her/himself, and then raped. The man, Hogg, uses the boy as his personal cum and piss bag while loaning the kid out to his friends and associates. Oh, by the way, Hogg shits and pisses on himself the way the rest of us choose to use a toilet bowl. And get this: the boy is a willing, engaged, and active participant in the relationship!

The boy, whose name we don't ever know because he speaks only one word to the other characters in the entire story of two-hundred pages, joins Hogg at the closing of one of his jobs and on the eve of another. On the new job, Hogg enlists the assistance of three associates to gang rape and brutally attack several women in one evening. The jobs end in an unexpected killing spree by one of the associates who is suffering from an infection that was caused by an impromptu, homemade Prince Albert (a body-piercing in the crown of the penis). The young narrator gets sold into sexual slavery, escapes, and reunites again with Hogg. All of this takes place in the context of a 48-hour period.

So why did I enjoy reading it? Let me first do something that no other reviewer will probably do: I admit that parts of the story sexually aroused me. What parts, you ask? I was aroused by the piss play and the cum-swallowing, very aroused. I'm not one for shit eating, pedophilia, rape and abuse of women and children. I want to be clear that I don't think shit eating and the rest of these actions are in any way on the same level, compatible, or connected. I do, however, love piss drinkers and cum swallowers. That being said, I did have to wade through some of the elaborate shit eating and the barrage of brutality that Delany throws at the reader to get to the other side where I knew he would have something that I enjoyed waiting for me. So let's get to the really controversial stuff (assuming shit eating isn't that controversial for you).

The very diligent and detailed description of pedophilia, rapes of women, and the abuses of women and children in the novel demand treatment in any review of the work, if, for nothing else, than to consider the implications for the writing and publishing of such a work within US society. First let me say that if you want to have a better understanding of some of Delany's creations in Hogg you should probably read some of his other work, like The Mad Man, Bread and Wine: An Erotic Tale of New York, The Motion of Light in Water: Sex and Science Fiction Writing in the East Village, and Times Square Red, Times Square Blue. In these works, you'll get to see what Delany is working with before he takes it out, beats you in the head with it, and then sticks it in your ears, ass, and mouth repeatedly in a seemingly never-ending torturous cycle of the meta-carnal (I just made up that word, but if you understand both parts you'll get what I mean by the compounding of them).

In those other works, you'll learn that on the personal side Delany has a thing for nasty, dirty motherfuckers. I mean that literally. From his work, you see he loves homeless men. Find a motherfucker with no shoes on, fingernails bitten to the meat, and a stench so bad that it makes your eyes water, with a layer of dirt an inch thick and you'll probably find Delany there sucking his dick. That leads me to my other observation of Delany, the man, through his work: Samuel R. Delany is a cocksucker. And I say that with love and affection for the man. His use of the word cocksucker and his creation of the iconic character, the cocksucker, in Hogg and The Mad Man, raises the cocksucker figure to the level of Jungian archetypes. When Delany talks about the cocksucker he's talking about himself. Therein lies the rub. Although only 10-years old, the narrator-boy in Hogg is really Delany. That's what makes this story not about pedophilia. Delany is not taking the perspective of those men who have sex with the boy. In fact, we, the readers, only know what it's like to desire the narrator-boy through the limited statements of some of the men in the story. And in those statements Delany does not give those characters their full voice. Instead we know what it means to desire these filthy, dirty, stinking men in graphic, precise detail through the narrator-boy's voice. Delany privileges the boy's voice by making him our narrator, thereby giving him a power and privilege the brutal men in the story don't have. The pedophile is disempowered by the boy's power to give voice to the story, to tell us what happened through his eyes despite the capacity for violence that the pedophile has. But that power exists because the boy, as I read him, is a manifestation of the man, Delany, who loves fingernail-biting, dirty ass men who love pissing and cuming in a man's mouth and all over a man's body.

What of the brutality against women? Here, Delany's skills as an artisan of the craft of writing fail him slightly. He's too heavy-handed with telling us, rather than showing us, what the brutality toward women is about. One of the first things that creative writing teachers tell their students is to *show* rather than *tell* character motivations. In one instance, Hogg makes this very awkwardly constructed speech of militant feminism laced with down-home folksy wisdom that hints at Delany's motives. Basically, Hogg says that if he was a woman he'd start killing every man he saw until there were none left. This is from a guy who gets paid to beat and fuck the shit out of women (literally) until they bleed, pee, and shit from their mouth. In a nutshell, Hogg explains his reasoning by saying that men hate women and that men aren't shit. He justifies what he does by saying that at least he's up front about his shit. He asserts the nobility of getting his hands dirty in the gender war rather than being a button pusher or lever puller. So what does this have to do with Delany using the story to make such a go of it in the brutality against women department? I believe it's because he wants us to choke on it. He wants us to be so sickened by the depravity and brutality that we literally choke on it. Because if we do, then he can confront us with the social brutality and violence against women that we conspire in or perpetrate everyday. You want to get upset and point the finger at Hogg, the rapist, misogynist, and batterer, then you better point the finger at yourself for conspiring with a society that engages in acts that have the same cumulative impact upon women and girls. You want to point the finger at Big Sambo, one of Delany's *Hogg* characters who has his daughter kept up in the shack with him so he can "fuck on her" and let others get a piece, then you have to look at yourself when you sit passively by and let the father of the bride "give" his daughter away to another man as though she were his own personal property. Delany is turning our brutality and hatred of women back on us and hoping we drown in it like a tsunami. He paints for us scenes that are so disturbing and jarring in their detail and explicated-ness because he doesn't want us to be able to shut our eyes or run away from the horror of our collective social selves. And remember it's the narrator-boy who make us watch and smell and hear it all—powerful.

The racial shit. Delany has his *cracker* (i.e. poor/working class, white, European, European-American—my usage, not Delany's) characters call every Black person around a nigger. It rolls off their tongues like it does off political comedian Paul Mooney's and—as Mooney would say—it makes their teeth just as white as his. These white folks are also fucking and getting fucked by niggers, loving and being loved by niggers. Delany juxtaposes mindless racist practice alongside intimate interracial contact that is, at times, loving, affectionate, and caring. Again, he allows Hogg to tell, rather than show us that crackers love niggers, as long as the niggers stay in line and don't get too uppity. If niggers do get uppity then crackers got to crack some nigger skulls to get things back in order, the social order of the US. Delany plays with his complex, monstrous creation, forcing it to show the absurdity of white supremacy and its manifestation, racism.

However troubling it is, this work is a must read. It is one of the most challenging works to consume because it's meant to be. Samuel R. Delany shows himself, again, to be an author and theorist of immense proportion as he confronts us with ourselves. I would, with honor, dump a load of cum and piss down Delany's throat. As my esteemed elder, I think he deserves no less. Having him suck my dick until he hits fluid would be an honor. But I doubt that would ever happen considering that I don't bite my nails, am never covered in dirt and funk, and have been too sanitized by education (there's tremendous class analysis in Delany's work). Nevertheless, I love my brother and I continue to submit myself to the challenge of his erotic fiction and writings in critical theory.

Thanks, Chip.

FETISH: FOR/OF WHOM?

One night, I participated in a conversation about sex at a dinner party in Brooklyn. This conversation was a planned discussion of sex as part of an issue of *NRG Magazine* on the topic of sex. The conversation created a space for me, as I often have such things happen, to develop my thinking on a topic by just talking aloud and witnessing what comes forth. This time I got to do some thinking on fetishism. Well, actually, my thinking carried me toward some insights about fetishism and fetishes.

I find it very telling that the term "fetish" and its attendant concept "fetishism" are used in two very distinct and seemingly unrelated areas of the Western patriarchal, body-phobic academy: anthropology and psycho-social sex research. Anthropologists use the term fetishism to describe a category of cultural practices by non-Western people. A fetish is an "inanimate object" to which non-Western indigenous peoples ascribe a spiritual significance usually through some process of ritual or consecration.

It is important to observe here that the concept "inanimate object" is itself loaded with Western cultural biases. In the West, what has been considered animate or alive has been very limited (as compared with non-Western cultural traditions) and delimited to those things that, for example, contain carbon-based molecules, engage in certain "biological activities" such as reproduction, respiration, and others. Objects, within the West, have had an even more powerful place while also existing in a much more fluid category. Objects are delineated in relation to the Subject, the Knower, the Thinker, and the Observer. So everything and everyone else can be an Object as I, the Subject, stand in relation to them, the Objects. This Subject-Object relationship has been a way for the West to distinguish itself from everything else, for men to distinguish themselves from everything else. In this context, human beings are not nature. They stand outside of nature or with nature around them and they observe it, or at least have the capacity to observe it. This capacity is, therefore, said to be object-ive.

As for a fetish, it can be a mask, statue, figurine, or other such object that is constructed to hold some power or force or value greater than that of the original elements that were used to construct the object. People who deal in the art and artifacts of non-Western indigenous people will frequently distinguish between pieces that are fetish pieces and those that are non-fetish pieces with the fetish pieces being more monetarily valuable because of the significance given to them by the cultural group that produced them.

A fetish in psychosocial sex research is usually considered a construction of the value or sexual meaning of something by an individual or group such that the object of the fetish carries more sexual charge or currency than it does for the general population or than it does in its everyday context. Well-known examples of fetishes include feet and underwear. With these two examples we can observe that feet and underwear (not lingerie) have little to moderate sexual force ascribed to them in the general population but among foot fetishists and underwear fetishists feet and underwear, respectively, generate considerable sexual excitement and arousal. A fetishist may engage in specific or deliberate activity in relation to the object of fetish such as a foot fetishist licking someone's bare feet or shoed feet or an underwear fetishist sniffing the clean or worn underwear of someone.

I find the conceptual space within which these two seemingly distant contexts for the concepts of "fetish" and "fetishism" meet interesting.

Fetishizing The Other

Much of Western scholarship in the last millennia has been a collection of epistemic practices that have had the result of fetishizing the Other. Everything that was non-Western was fetishized. Anthropology and archeology are fields of study and fetish. Antiquity and aboriginal museums and museum exhibits are fetish palaces. Anthropology, archeology, and the museums that have been built because of them have catered to the fetish needs of Western populations that desire non-Western people as objects (as opposed to Subjects).

We, the Other and the Objects of Western fetishism, have had our skulls, hips, and dicks measured and categorized by the West in the name of science while in the service of Western fetishism. The West has fetishized our lips, eyes, and skin. We have become the fetish itself as international tourism to Africa, Southeast Asia, South America, and the Caribbean has satiated the lusts and desires of European and US markets for subaltern/tri-continental/Indigenous flesh.

The Political Economy of the Western Fetish of The Other

Capitalism and fetishism are lovers. Capitalism provides the supply channel through which Western fetishists/capitalists gain access to the raw materials of our bodies. Whether within international markets or within their sovereign, local markets, Western fetishist-capitalists extract from our bodies, be they colored, feminine, queer, de-formed, and/or masculine bodies, the necessary social materials that produce the fetishized woman, or the fetishized native, or the fetishized faggot, or the fetishized rent boy, or the fetishized savage, etc.

The West then uses us—our bodies wrapped in various social materials—as fetishes (in the anthropological sense of the word), performing rituals with/to/on us that empower the Western social community. The West is empowered and empowers itself as a result of fetishizing us. Capitalism, science, and art are means through which the West fetishizes us—The Other. The lynched bodies of African men throughout the United States (lynching happened in more places in the US than just the southern part of the US) were totem for the cultural village we call the United States. The atomic energy-scorched bodies of the men, women, and children of Hiroshima and Nagasaki were talismans used to conjure the power of Western colonial power/force.

Fetishism as an Act of Power and Privilege

In both the anthropological and the psychosocial sex research approach, fetishism is an act of power and privilege (even though fetishism in Western sex research has often been portrayed as neurotic and obsessive, and therefore uncontrollable, pathological, and a sign of a weak ego). In the indigenous context, one has to be privileged enough to have the knowledge to create a "fetish" and powerful enough to "animate" the fetish.

In the sexual context, one exercises (whether one realizes this or not) a level of privilege to fetishize something or someone because to fetishize something or someone you have to first act from the social position of a Subject (an autonomous, independent entity distinct/disconnected/alienated from the other—the object of fetish) rather than an object (part of the environment). The fetishist's desire is organized around an object that is outside of the fetishist. The fetishist exercises social power or social resource to construct the object of fetish into a fetish to which the fetishist can have access.

The West (Europe, the US, Canada, and Australia, and apartheid-governed South Africa) has exercised its privilege and power in service of its fetish with the rest of us. It has kept us close enough to touch and taste. And our exploitation has been a form of fetish practice—a global kink scene with all the accoutrements of bondage-domination, sadomasochism play.

DO YOU REMEMBER?

do you remember
what they told us
they told us
you are having sex
with everyone he ever
had sex with
and you wondered why
the sex didn't feel better
last longer
with all these other motherfuckers

in the picture

do you remember
do you remember
do you remember
what they told us
what they told us
what they told us
they told us
the consistent and proper use of a condom
drastically reduces your risk
of HIV infection
a latex sleeve reduced
our sexual risk
while we could be
jailed for the sex
we were having
our sex was pathologized, demonized, ostracized
our sex was filled
with self-hatred, guilt, shame
objectification, envy, and rage
they called that safe
how the fuck is a condom
going to protect you from
a nigga that hates himself
and hates you for loving him
how's a condom going to
protect you from wanting
that motherfucker's dick
up in you in the first place

do you remember
do you remember
do you remember
what they told us
what they told us
what they told us
they told us
HIV is the virus that causes AIDS
yet they had no causes

only correlates
they made the AIDS definition
and infected HIV with it
then said HIV causes AIDS
what about the cause of HIV
where'd that come from
why did it come
at that time
did they tell you
green monkeys, africans, haitians
were targeted
but did you find the answers
where are the answers now

do you remember
do you remember
do you remember
what they told us
what they told us
what they told us
they told us
AIDS is the leading cause of death among...
AIDS is leading the cause of death
like Martin Luther King or Farrakhan
leading marches on Washington
like Caesar Chavez working for
economic social justice in the fields
like Sojourner Truth and Harriet Tubman
working for women's rights and human rights
like complex Angela D
struggling against the prison industry
AIDS is a freedom fighter
leading the cause of death

do you remember
do you remember
do you remember
what they told us
what they told us
what they told us

they told us
AIDS equals Death
and thousands of people
who passed third grade math
prepared to die
so many people got ready
to die of AIDS
there wasn't enough
preparation to live with HIV
T cells got higher viewer ratings
than the Cosby Show and Cheers combined
T cells went up and down
more than park trade
on a dick at 2 am
in the morning

do you remember
do you remember
do you remember
what they told us
what they told us
what they told us
they told us
only immediate family
may be present
and we were discarded
along with precious
pieces of people
we loved as family
cared for as family
when family was neither
immediate nor familial

do you remember
do you remember
do you remember
what they told us
what they told us
what they told us
they told us

he has 3-6 months
to live
and they tried to get us
to stuff a life
into the container of
one moment
one action

do you remember
do you remember
do you remember
what they told us
what they told us
what they told us
they told us
here are your test results
and we were scared
shitless
because there was
that one time
I knew I shouldn't
but that nigga had
me open
and he looked ok
he was clean
didn't have any
cuts, bruises, open sores, swollen nodes or glands,
scaly skin, drawn cheeks,
blotchy spots, really low muscle mass

do you remember
do you remember
do you remember
what they told us
what they told us
what they told us
they told us
your test came back positive
and life stopped
and started again

all our worst fears
became true
we wept
on our knees
on the floor
in a fetal position
knees pressed against
our beating hearts
But we lived
and we died
But we lived
and we died
But we lived
and we died

do you remember
what they told us
what they told us

what they told us

(GYM) BODIES THAT MATTER
AND WHY

We are well within the "fitness revolution." It's a revolution to increase muscle mass, decrease body fat, and remove every unsightly blemish plaguing our skin. The revolution touches all of our lives in some way. Through gym memberships, diet pills, workout videos, home training equipment, diet books, and celebrity endorsed, over-the-counter acne medication, we are inundated with more "fitness" material than New Orleans was with water.

Many of us, particularly in urban centers around the US, are encouraged to sculpt and texture our bodies to mimic as closely as possible particular molds of physicality. These molds differ for men and women but the emphasis on increasing muscle mass and decreasing body fat while also limiting blemishes exists for both sexes. Anyone else, e.g., trannies, intersexed, is also encouraged to conform to these standardized molds. In fact, those who, for whatever reason, fall outside of mainstream forms of sex identities—i.e., male and female—had better do their damnedest to conform to whichever form of sex that they most closely resemble or with which they most closely associate.

Fat and blemishes have become evils unto themselves. People who have what is considered excessive fat become identified with the fat that they carry so that we call the people fat and they may during moments of self-disclosure call themselves fat. The noun, fat—the substance housed in and out of our bodies, becomes the adjective, fat—a description of a person carrying more fat than we as a society have deemed appropriate.

Skin blemishes (including acne, vitiligo, dandruff, and eczema) disturb our expectations for smoothness and seamlessness. We associate them with oiliness or dryness. They remind us of our reptilian heritage and we are ashamed. Every year millions of over the counter medications and treatments, prescription medications, and cosmetics are purchased to shelter the world from the challenge to perfection that our skin produces, thereby sheltering us from the disapproving, disgusted gaze of society.

At the intersection of skin color, culture, gender/sex, class, and sexuality, these forces play out in very interesting ways. We live in a very toxic environment in the West. What we eat, breathe, and drink as well as where we live and what we do for income all have an impact upon how fat and blemished our bodies are. Racism and classism manage skin color and class to (de)limit the options we have in terms of what we eat, drink, and breathe as well as where we work and the kind of work we do. Capitalism manages our appetites to turn the food preferences we have, because of culture or historical legacy, into agents of our own demise. Additives, preservatives, chemical enhancers, and hormones in our foods and beverages have engineered the colonization of our bodies so that we are no longer in control of our bodies. Obesity, asthma, hypoglycemia, diabetes, cancer, and hypertension are all manifestations of the dietary imperialism and environmental toxicity in which we live.

Capitalism has molded our bodies to fit the needs of the economy— making working class bodies, service sector bodies, information technology bodies, knowledge worker bodies, etc. If you sit at a desk for 10 hours a day, your body is going to look very different from someone who stands while making hamburgers and fries for 8 hours a day from someone who cleans hotel rooms for 8 hours a day from someone who sells her/his body for 12 hours a day from someone who picks grapes or harvests lettuce for 10 hours a day. But all of our bodies are in service to the wealth creation of a small group of individuals who are at the top of the capitalism pyramid.

For those of us whose labor doesn't mold our bodies into the hard muscle, low fat objects of aesthetic beauty touted in mass media and popular culture, we are encouraged to purchase gym memberships, home workout videos/equipment, diet books, supplements, etc. to build the better body. Capitalism wins again while we lose—lose our fat, our shame, our money, and our feelings of inadequacy. Capitalists count profits while we count calories. We are encouraged to explore and confront our relationship with food while avoiding examination of our relationship with a toxic environment brought about by capitalist moneyed interests and labor conditions that supplant healthy bodies through work conditions that make our bodies either frail and weak or stiff and weak.

Then there are the little dirty secrets that we don't like to talk about in polite conversation such as: bulimia and anorexia among women AND men, the abuse of colonics for the purposes of weight loss, steroid use among weight trainers (particularly, but not exclusively, among HIV positive gay men), stomach stapling, liposuction, etc. We may be willing to gossip about these things when it involves a "celebrity" but when it's about us or that hot someone across the room who we hope is attracted to us, we oftentimes remove it from our consciousness.

We're encouraged to crave the toned, muscled, and/or low fat among us. We're encouraged to believe that our desires to be and our desires to have those individuals are a natural manifestation of preference and desire. But how do we really know? Under layers upon layers of corporate messages about what is desirable, valuable, and attractive, how can any of us know for sure that what we find sexy, desirable, valuable, or attractive, or for that matter, undesirable, unattractive, or unappealing about ourselves or about others is a product of our authentic, indigenous preferences? When we decide we're going to the gym, or we're gonna get trim, toned, sculpted, muscled, what role are we playing in the oppression of others? In the oppression of ourselves?

Is there a form of physical culture that is unencumbered by capitalist, racist, classist, and sexist interests? If so, what would it feel like to practice it? What would loving ourselves physically, emotionally, spiritually, and socially look like within that physical culture? How would our choices in sex partners and lovers be different?

These are important questions for us to ponder in the climate within which we live with thin bois trying to get big (meaning muscled), small girls trying to get phat (meaning thick asses and big breasts), big bois and girls trying to get trim (meaning getting toned and tight) and few of us trying to get free of the oppressive social order that has us in bondage.

When I was 14, I was introduced to Tai Chi Chuan and Yoga. Both of these practices come from a very different kind of physical culture. In Tai Chi Chuan and Yoga, the objective is not to get toned or to get cuts or to bulk up one's muscles. Tai Chi Chuan and Yoga practitioners are interested in the cultivation of the inner Self through exercises that incorporate the physical body, the emotional self, the will, the energetic body, and the breath. Within these systems, health or fitness is assessed through an appreciation for the multiple dimensions of human personhood, i.e., mind, body, and spirit. The very young to the very old can and do practice Tai Chi Chuan and Yoga. Practitioners look at balance, harmony, coordination of thought, emotion and movement, lessening of the ego, and direction and extension of one's will as examples of development.

There are a number of alternative physical cultures and practices. Tai Chi Chuan and Yoga are just two examples. When more of us explore the alternatives, we may come just that much closer to a truly liberated society.

HOW BODIES FIT INTO
OPPRESSION/LIBERATION

A major part of the grassroots, mass movement struggle against Jim Crow involved an embodied mobilization. People put their bodies on the line (e.g., picketing, sit-ins, integrating lunch counters, marching, etc.) or removed their bodies from the line (e.g., boycotting). Perhaps we might be served by asking ourselves what would an embodied mobilization against the sexism, homo-hatred, and body fascism of "no fats, no fems" look like. Maybe it would look like boycotting the gym. Maybe it would look like dressing in drag in public space. Maybe it would look like glamorizing (i.e., making the subject/focus/feature of discourse) the rotund belly on our web sites rather than 6-pack abs.

One additional thing the civil rights movement has taught me is the problematic role of iv(or)y tower intellectuals and iv(or)y tower intellectualism in liberatory struggle. They were not the sparks that started the movement, nor the flames that kept the movement going. It was instead the kids at Shaw and Howard Universities, North Carolina A&T, and other places who were willing to get their hands dirty and lips bloody on the frontlines of the struggle.

I say that to say that intellectual gymnastics can be cute. As a PhD, I know their value and place. But as an activist, I also know the value of putting one's body on the line—literally not literarily, on the line. Let me be clear, I'm not pu-puing the value and role of the intellectual in liberatory struggle. In fact, what I am calling for is a rigorous embodiment of liberatory struggle by intellectuals in the context of "no fats, no fems." Where are the Che Gueveras, Frantz Fanons, and Angela Davises in the liberatory struggle with "no fats, no fems?" What would putting our bodies on the line in service of that struggle look like from a radical, critical perspective? Are those of us who fancy ourselves intellectual and activist living up to those standards and, if not, to what standards are we evaluating and critiquing our work?

At the point at which you decide to place another "look at my gym-processed abs/body" pic on your website alongside some text that most of your readers either don't read (properly) or can't understand, after numerous attempts in the past to do so, I believe you are contributing to, rather than critiquing, the body fascism that exists. Additionally, at the point at which you choose not to say to your blog readers, "Hey stupids, you're demonstrating the same cult of abs mentality that I'm trying to critique in my work. Either get a clue or stop reading/posting on my blog," you are opting for celebrity or at least congeniality over being the force for social change that you claim as your inspiration.

Likewise, former Black gay activist turned commentator Keith Boykin will forever be a superficial version of a social justice activist as long as he experiences a paralysis of analysis around body politics, his own and those of others. His site reads as soft core porn, a tits and ass site, with lukewarm social commentary for those who want social justice-lite edutainment. His lack of critical, public examination of the way in which his light-skin privilege and gym-processed body privilege operate to make him digestible and marketable in mainstream media, by gay bois and others, further complicates him as a force for social justice and fashions him more as a pop media commodity to be bought and sold just as his ancestors were during slavery.

Until men who were once skinny boys who felt uncomfortable with their bodies choose to dismantle the system of body fascism that we all live within rather than trying to soothe past wounds by becoming that thing they most desired when they were a kid—but not really achieving it—those men will suffer from a flawed analysis of oppression and a vulnerable articulation of social justice.

Until men with gym-processed bodies come out of the closet about other aspects of their bodies, e.g., asthma, HIV, hypertension, chronic halitosis, alcoholism, etc., they will continue to be collaborators in their own objectification. And there are reasons why they remain in the closet about these things. Imagine, for example, how an HIV-infected, gym-processed body is read by the public, not (simply) as a hot body but a body that is being "kept up" in the midst of the virus. By remaining in the closet about HIV, the gym-processed body can be socially airbrushed into acceptability.

If I can hold white folks accountable as social justice allies and demand that they do certain things as allies in the name of social justice (e.g., be silent and listen periodically, take a secondary but supportive role to a person of color, utilize their resources and privilege to advance a social justice objective without taking any credit, etc.), then I must be equally willing to hold ab-bois accountable as social justice allies as well.

If you have emotional/social stuff you need to work out by going to the gym and you also want to be a social justice ally, fine. Don't put your abs on your web site because it will not have the same impact as you intend. Manage your social currency with an appreciation for how it functions in the real world, not just in the world of ideas.

I know this work is hard. I struggle with it myself. But I've learned how important these issues are in the real lives of the real people in our communities. For those of you City Chat callers in NY, this story may sound familiar. I called the City Chat phone party line and purposely stated in my outgoing message that I wanted to meet ugly, unattractive men. I did so for two reasons: (1) I generally get bored with the monotonous, monkey-see-monkey-do sameness of the messages callers create on the party line. The messages are filled with the same clichés—"No fats, no fems," "Only on-point niggas hit me up," "Have your shit tight if you wanna hit me up," etc. I wanted to hear something different so I did something different; and (2) I wanted to explore my thoughts, feelings, and values regarding this supposed link between physical appearance, attraction, and sex.

If you know anything about these party lines, you know that everyone says they are looking for the dime piece and everyone complains that there are no dime pieces on the line and many ecstatically proclaim their status as a dime piece. What I experienced by creating my outgoing message was hilarious and enlightening. Some brothers contacted me and asked me why I would want someone unattractive and suggested it was because I was probably unattractive and couldn't do any better.

When I arbitrarily contacted brothers, some were offended since I stated that I wanted unattractive brothers. They didn't feel they were unattractive and felt insulted that I contacted them given my preference. When I told them that it was just a preference and not something that I rigidly held to and that they could be attractive and I would still fuck with them, they were still put off because they felt by pursuing an interaction with me they were admitting to or claiming being unattractive. In other words, by getting with someone who had a preference for unattractive people, they become unattractive people. I wonder if the converse and inverse are also the case.

A few brothers contacted me and were in doubt about whether they were attractive or unattractive and thought that by interacting with me their status might be affected. This shit was deep to me, not only because it called into question the social construction called attractiveness but also because it demonstrated how these dynamics play out in such intimate ways, sometimes in the context of just two people.

In the past I have most definitely had sex and sought out sex with people whom I felt weren't attractive to me and/or who didn't possess any of the socially defined, attractive physical appearances. I've done so for many reasons: because I knew the sex would be good and I wasn't willing to sacrifice good sex just because someone wasn't my idea or society's idea of attractive; because I knew they were getting off on the fact that they felt I was more attractive then they were and that got me off in return; or because I was really, really horny and they were there. All of those reasons are just that, reasons, not excuses.

People's desire clouds and colors their assessments about what others say and do. Empirical studies have been conducted that demonstrate that when a person's appearance is most in line with what is considered conventionally attractive (symmetry of face, skin tone, body frame, etc.) what they say is believed more than those whose appearance is not as conventionally attractive and as a result people treat them differently, e.g., are more willing to assist and help them, more receptive to their requests, etc.

In Black community, this has also played out in terms of skin color. Generate a list of people who have been designated as African-American or Black leaders on a national or international scale over the last 100 years and you will find that the majority are male and light to brown skinned.

The fact that someone may prefer light skin or brown skin on his or her sexual partners is not the issue. The fact that that preference is transferred into their social, political, or economic allegiances is a political, social, and economic act with real consequences for people. It means that we frequently are stuck with individuals, projects, and organizations that cannot provide us with much more than window-dressing while the substantive issues of our community go unaddressed.

On the issue of economics, when sex party promoters, in an effort to cater to the bias, preferences, and prejudices of the mainstream or the masses, create a "no fats, no fems" policy that they believe will be interpreted by consumers as a "hot boy party," they are reinforcing, supporting, and promoting the belief that men who are fat or fem (as though fat and fem are these exact terms with exact meanings that we all hold) are not desirable, have no right to have sex with non-fat, non-fem men, and are threats to the sexual and erotic environment of a sex party if they are present. In the same way, white-owned businesses during Jim Crow segregation reinforced, supported, and promoted the belief that Black folks had no right to eat alongside white folks and that they were a threat to the comfort and enjoyment of white folks if they were present.

When the sex party promoters say, in their defense, that they are not creating these rules of desire they are merely responding to them as good business people, they are ignoring their role as fellow human beings. They choose to give up their collective and social responsibility to make a buck. Capitalists have done that since the beginning of modern capitalism, i.e., the slave trade. There is nothing new about that. I disagree with the capitalist premise that all products start with a real/pure desire/need. In fact, I believe one aspect of capitalism is the production/manufacturing of *perceived* need/desire. There's a whole lot of shit on the market we don't need but we're encouraged through marketing to desire it and believe we need it.

Sex party promoters are not the only capitalists doing it today. In my years of socializing in "Black gay" environments, I have observed that too many of the individuals with 100,000 page views per day sites, book tours, co-editorships on anthologies, and claims to the title "leader" or "spokesman" are folks who are not qualified or are terribly mediocre. When I read their analysis of the issues affecting Black folks and Black queer folks, or lack thereof, I am thoroughly unimpressed. These people tend to also be the people who are on many people's I-wish-I-could-fuck list. They are too often given a pass on the mediocrity of their thinking, strategies, and actions because they are "cute."

I'm not even saying these folks are attractive, at least in the way I conceive attractive. But they conform to certain criteria that make it easy for people to digest them as sexual beings, e.g. body frame, skin tone, level of masculinity/effeminacy, etc. The interesting thing is, and I just realized this as I began to write this sentence, that their thinking, strategies, and actions are equally easy to digest. They don't require much of their audience, sexually or intellectually in how they get into them. I think what also makes them attractive in "Black gay community" is that they don't require us to do much work toward our liberation.

When the only choices available on the national scene are Phil Wilson of the Black AIDS Institute and Keith Boykin, of www.keithboykin.com, on one side and Cleo Manago of Amassi Inc. and Black Men's Xchange on the other side, something is terribly wrong. Yes, HIV/AIDS has limited much of our options in the way of critical voices of liberation and struggle but our own lookism and sexism has also limited those options. We have excluded certain voices in the main square of "Black gay community" by the degree to which the appearance of the message or the messenger has been pleasing to our sensibilities and our desire to not have to work hard.

The "no fats, no fems" policy at the sex party is representative of a laziness around desire, values, critical thinking, and socially responsible action. And it isn't policy for certain sex parties; it is (implicit/explicit) policy at most parties and the expectation of many people who either attend the parties or consider attending. I'm speaking from experience as a former sex party organizer who has talked with numbers of party promoters and attendees. My party, The Workshop, had a deliberate non-discriminatory admittance policy. I felt that party attendees, as responsible adults, could decide for themselves with whom they wished to interact in the context of the party. I did not feel a need to spoon-feed them certain types of bodies or to assume that they were only interested in certain types of bodies.

I believe anytime you are "enterprising," which really means exploiting and using, a demographic/market whether economically as a capitalist business owner, intellectually as a capitalist scholar/ researcher, spiritually as a capitalist religious leader, etc. you are socially irresponsible, counter-revolutionary, and ethically bankrupt as a human being. The capitalist mindset is by definition exploitative and therefore socially irresponsible. Having said that, I do not expect most sex party promoters to do anything differently. They are among the most parasitic, narcissistic, socially unconscious people whom I've encountered.

The focus of my work for the last seven years has been the creation of solutions to these issues. I've been working on several tools, strategies, and actions with a number of folks to create appropriate interventions. What I've learned over those years is that what can be done requires work, internal and external, requires a community of support to act as mirror, coach, mentor, and companion, requires the involvement of the body, mind, and spirit, requires commitment, authenticity, and integrity, and requires an acceptance of the unknown, not knowing, chaos, complexity, and the loss of perceived control. More importantly, we must have the will to imagine and work toward a more socially just world, a more empowered way of living, and a more humane way of being in relationship with life.

PUTTING THE DOWN LOW
(BLACK) MAN TO BED

Let's begin to ask some thoughtful questions about the assumptions underneath the messages that continue to be rammed down our throats like an inexperienced, incompetent dumb dick with regard to the concept of the "Down Low Brotha." There are several fatally incorrect assumptions that underlie the discussion of "DL phenomenon" in popular culture:

1.   The terms gay, straight, heterosexual, homosexual, and bisexual provide reliable and relevant information about a given person's emotional, sexual, or social behavior—past, present, or future.

• The sexual identity categories (gay, straight, heterosexual, homosexual, bisexual) that have been developed by white folks for white folks are fatally flawed. They don't mean shit. Too many ill-informed Black folks—who are still only two weeks away from the plantation and therefore yet to have developed a sense of personal sexual liberation—have adopted these categories for themselves and placed them onto others. Too often people have made decisions based upon assumptions that were rooted in a belief in the validity of these categories when in fact the categories are meaningless beyond the socially constructed meanings that have been applied to them for political and economic reasons.

2.   Black men who have sex with men and women without informing the women of their homosexual sexual activity are responsible for the increase in seroconversion rates among Black women.
   • This is a sexist and racist assumption. It disempowers Black women sexually, intellectually, and morally as well as demonizes Black men while ignoring the systemic and structural forces at work in a racist, sexist, heterosexist, erotophobic, and classist society that places Black women and Black men at greater risk of poverty, death, and disease.

3.   Men who have sex with men and women without informing the women of their homosexual sexual activity are deceitful and underhanded.
   • Personal disclosure in relationships is a very complex and intricate dance that occurs over a period of time and is based in the reciprocity of truth and understanding, sharing and accepting. A number of factors influence the timing by which someone shares any piece of personal, intimate information with someone in an evolving relationship. The decision not to share is not necessarily tied to deceit or malice. It may be tied to the level of intimacy or trust felt in a relationship as well as other factors. The decision to have sex is not necessarily as involved as the act of disclosure for some people, particularly men. Consequently, the decision to have sex can be made and is oftentimes made way before the decision to disclose personal history/information. Add to those circumstances the potential social consequences, i.e., the costs of disclosing/sharing personal history/information, and the probability that sex will happen before the sharing of certain personal histories is magnified. It would further our understanding of the social circumstances of

these women's seroconversion to find out the levels of relationship (e.g., one-night stand, dating, long term relationship, marriage, etc.) the women were in when they seroconverted.

4. Men who have sex with men and women without informing the women of their homosexual sexual activity use the phrase DL to designate their identities and/or their sexual behavior with men.
  • In general, the men who classify their sexual behavior with men as "DL" tend to be men who have sex exclusively with men NOT men who have sex with men and women. DL in that context is an indicator of masculine performance and the ability/capacity of a man to enjoy heterosexual-identity privilege in general society. Among men who exclusively have sex with men, DL status is oftentimes a form of social currency like having a big dick, six-pack abs, youth, or a good job. Please understand "exclusive" in this context to mean a general tendency of sexual behavior over someone's entire lifetime. More often than not, men who have sex with men and women without informing the women of their same-sex behavior identify as straight or heterosexual because in 90% of their life they have conformed to the social standards set forth for straight or heterosexual men. Because they're everyday life does not conform to the stereotypes and socially constructed "story" of what a "gay man" should be, do, feel, or look like, there is no rational reason for them to take on a socially stigmatized identity that has no real meaning to them. So there's no "coming out" that they need to do or any further "being real with themselves." They are who and what they are. The problems are in the social definitions that have been constructed and attempted in referring to them.

5. DL behavior/identity is specific to Black men.
  • In the 1960s, Laud Humphreys conducted a study in the Midwest of the United States that described the secret same-sex practice of middle-class, married white men in public restrooms. The title of the published study was *Tearoom Trade: Impersonal Sex in Public Places.*

6. The prevention solution for Black women seroconverting is for Black men who have sex with men and women to identify as gay or inform their female sexual partners that they are having sex with men.
  • If knowing that a man slept with men was the solution to preventing seroconversion, then no man who has sex with men

would have ever seroconverted because that knowledge would be readily available when sex was initiated. The prevention solution is sexual empowerment and sexual agency. Those solutions take work, intentionality, effort, courage, commitment, and struggle. It means not taking for granted certain comforting assumptions (assumptions which a lot of men who have sex with men have had to do away with in the face of HIV/AIDS) such as assuming you have sex safely with someone just because you think he is straight or clean or whatever. If you want to know, get tested together several times over a 9-month period before having condomless sex and continue to get tested thereafter. Or decide not to ever have condomless sex unless you are intending to have a baby.

• I don't think the "straight" world is really aware of the emotional, psychological, and logistical impact HIV/AIDS has had on the way men who have sex with men approach the act of sex—all the work that we do in confronting all the social messages about disease, health, responsibility, etc. Guess what? Heterosexually-identified folks have to do it too but, for the most part, they haven't been because they've been falsely comforted by the belief that there are straight people over here and gay people over there and one world doesn't impact the other when it comes to sex. Heterosexually-identified folks could fuck without fear while the rest of us had to fuck in the face of our fears because, ultimately, human beings are gonna fuck—biological and erotic imperative.

• Certain people want to blame the badass DL man for taking away their sexual privilege as straight people to fuck without fear and fuck without responsibility. They want to ignore the thousands of children who are conceived without consideration for their preparation as productive parents. They just want to fuck without fear and fuck without responsibility and the big bad DL man took that away by reminding them that they have to be conscious and committed and vigilant in their sexual health and empowerment and that shit is too fucking much like work. How is someone to enjoy sex while having to think and do all that? Exactly.

7. In a scenario where a Black man who has sex with men and women has condomless sexual intercourse with a Black woman and he does not tell her that he has sex with men, the Black man is more responsible for the potential seroconversion of the Black woman than she is and

therefore he is a murderer, predator, deviant, and enemy of the Black community.
- This assumption is too stupid to warrant comment.

8.   HIV+ Black men who have sex with men and women without informing women of their same-sex practice exclusively choose Black women to have condomless sex.
- This is another example of racism. We would love to ignore the fact that Black men fuck all kinds of women. So why aren't they responsible for the seroconverting among those women? We would love to ignore the fact that other women aren't seroconverting at the same rates as Black women. So what the fuck is particular to Black women that they are seroconverting? It is not Black men. Black women have sex with all kinds of men.

There are a number of reasons why Black men don't talk about their same-sex practice that have never been explored in popular discourse. Black men and women carry the historical legacy and the remnants of slave mentality. Slave sexuality was often a private matter, personal and communal, because of the sexual exploitation that they experienced through the forced breeding processes engineered by white slaveholders. An enslaved African's attempts to keep his/her sexual desires and choices of sexual behavior rooted in personal preference were acts of resistance and defiance against a brutal system of sexual exploitation and oppression.

Black men and women also carry a historical legacy from our African roots. At least as far back as colonial Africa, Africans have held matters of sexual behavior as personal and private to the individual or engaged parties. While there was no concept of sexual identity per se, in many communities there was/is acknowledgement of a multiplicity of sexual behaviors, including same-sex practice, that members of the community might perform that Africans have traditionally chosen not to translate into sexual identity categories like the ones developed by white folks. Married women and men could/do engage in what we in the West would consider same-sex practice without experiencing social pressure to "identify" or "disclose" as gays, homosexuals, or bisexual. Such calls for sexual identification and sexual information, as responsible acts, are quite contemporary and quite Western.

Being responsible does not lie in any one particular action that a person may take but rather in her/his intent, consciousness, and awareness in taking any action. The Black community would be better off if European-American capitalist interests didn't simultaneously consider it both a threat to European-American society and a source of cultural and economic exploitation. No amount of closet clearing or closet cleaning on the part of Black men who have sex with men and women is gonna necessarily address those underlying issues.

Having said all of that, all Black men who have sex with men as well as women and don't openly discuss their sexual practices are not necessarily exercising freedom of sexuality. While I agree there is definitely some agency in their decisions to not disclose, I also believe that the decision to not disclose is tied to a general sense of sexual repression that all Black folks in this country endure either because the laws and social codes of this society admonish the kind of sex that gets their pussies wet or their dicks hard or because they have internalized these admonishments to the degree that they feel they must live up to certain conservative standards of healthy sexual behavior that are not authentically their own. In fact, most of United States society is in the closet. Read Kinsey's studies of sexuality in the United States.

The messages that Black men specifically receive are profound. Consider this. Remember the statistic that 1 in 4 or 3 in 4 (I can't remember now) Black men between the ages of something and something are under the authority of law enforcement (prison, jail, parole, probation, etc.)? Ok, let's say it's 1 in 4. That means that if you're not under the authority of law enforcement, you are one of the 3 in 4. Subtract from that the numbers of Black men who are not college-educated. You have about 2 in 25 now. Let's say you look halfway decent. You have degrees, a good job or you own a business or you have wealth potential. Now put yourself in the Black community where because of patriarchy, sexism, and European male supremacy, sisters are told that you are the "thing" that will complete their picture. Can you image the enormous pressure you would experience in that context to perform, to be the man? Now, suppose, in addition to all of that, you have a desire to be with another man sexually, emotionally, or both—desires that you may not have realized or allowed yourself to realize until you were 20, 30, 40, or 50 or until you have two children or a very invested wife or a mortgage or 6-figure salary, etc.

Where do you begin to tell your partner that the American Dream that the two of you have constructed for yourselves has this other emerging storyline? That's not my story but it is a story. My story is much more complex than that story and blows much of the popular discussion of DL Black men out the window. I had a 10-year relationship with a woman. A month into our relationship she knew that I had had sex with other males when I was 16/17. She challenged me to clarify what my desires/needs were at that time and we spent ten years dealing with the consequences of that challenge. When I made the decision to finally end the relationship so that she could have the possibility of being happy in a way that she would never have had with me and so that I could do the same, she was hurt, enraged, and devastated. She wanted to keep working at it. She wanted to continue to live through the emotional upheavals, fears, jealousies, depressions, etc. I helped her to raise two children that her str8 ex-husband had abandoned emotionally. I had seen her go from working at a small administrative job to enjoying a 6-figure salary, a home worth nearly a million dollars, an SUV, etc., etc., etc. I don't take credit for her success but I do honor the contributions that we both made to each other's development over the ten years.

Where we had conflict in the relationship was not the sex I was having with other men while we were together (and yes she knew I was having sex with men). The conflict was in the fact that I wanted to be in emotionally intimate relationships with other men and that was not something with which she could comfortably deal. But she wanted to stay together regardless. Now some would be quick to call her weak or say she had low self-esteem for wanting to continue to be in the situation. What I'm trying to share is my experience of the situation. The complexity of my experience in that relationship is rendered completely irrelevant in the public discourse of what it means to be a Black man in a relationship with a Black woman while also desiring other men. This stuff can't be boiled down to neat little stereotypes of Black men or Black women. What's happening in people's relationships is a whole lot more complex and human.

I remember one of the participants in a research study I conducted talking about how he was challenged by the heterosexual dynamics that played out in his relationships with women even though he openly identified as a Black gay man and never had sex with any of these women. The same interactions that were common to men and women who were in sexual relationships often popped up in his relationships with women. The complexities of human interaction challenge the simplicity that gets artificially constructed and fed to us in the media.

One contribution to the solution: we need to educate ourselves a lot more. I'm not talking about someone informing you of his or her sexual behavior; that's another issue. I'm talking about stepping out of the general ignorance that most of us have grown up in about life, living, what's going on in the world. Too many of us get what we know from the entertainment and media industries. There are too few of us who are reading past the sensational novel/book of the month or the daily newspaper. Too few of us step outside of our comfort zones to explore, examine, and understand the margins of society or those who have been pushed to the margins of society or to recognize when we are considered the margins of society.

As many of us begin to take these actions, it would be productive to have members of the community support us rather than demonize or pathologize us. I'm often reminded of a statement I heard once, "How can I tell you about me if I don't know who me is right now?" My question to us is, "How do we create a safe space for each of us to find out who we are while also maintaining a safe space for those around us to continue to love us and be loved by us?" I don't think we do that by finger pointing, scapegoating, or denying and hiding our light.

Personally, I have made some hard decisions about who, how, when, and to what degree I choose to love so I'm in no way interested in denying the responsibility that other men have to make equally difficult decisions nor am I interested in denying the responsibility that women have to make equally difficult decisions. Yet, I see as heterosexism and homophobia the distinguishing of the men who lie, deceive, and otherwise mislead their female partners to have sex with men from the men who lie, deceive, and otherwise mislead their female partners to have sex with women. Women know that men have done these things for centuries. Therefore, the decision to have sex without a condom is riddled with a lot of stuff including a tolerance for the possibility of infidelity as long as it's with other women as well as a belief in the exclusive normality of heterosexuality.

There's no way that I could defend deceitful behavior. Deceitful behavior doesn't warrant my defense. Nor can I attack a sister for wanting to have or for having unprotected sex. I can't attack brothers for that either. Sex feels better without the use of a condom. I will however criticize those forces in our society that would demonize any of us for our attempts to express our divinely given urges/needs in a society that is violently opposed to our sexual liberation and empowerment.

I will work for sexual liberation and empowerment. I do that through my work in Black Funk: by committing my time, energy, creativity, financial resources, and any other resources to that struggle; by not settling for the easy answers to complex questions even when giving the public the easy answer would probably be more financially profitable for me and while the more complex answer challenges people to do some things they may not readily want to do.

HOW WE USE THE MASTER'S TOOLS TO DISMANTLE OUR HOUSE

In August 2003, New York City was host to two different Black Pride celebration schedules. In addition to the schedule of the original Black Pride NYC organizers, a Brooklyn-based social service organization, People of Color in Crisis (POCC), organized a collection of events they called Pride in the City. The emergence of this second, competing schedule was a source of concern and confusion for folks. A month after this fiasco, I penned the following analysis.

Black Pride NYC and its host organization Black Pride NYC, Inc. is basically a funder. Its events, such as Black Pride NYC, are supposed to generate money that is put back into the community in the form of scholarships, fellowships, grants, and donations to social service and community-based organizations. The events have never made enough money for Black Pride NYC, Inc. to make any substantial contributions in any of these areas. Black Pride NYC, Inc. continues to have debts outstanding from previous years' events. The leadership of Black Pride NYC, Inc. is primarily male.

POCC is a social service organization providing services to the LGBT/Q community (mainly Black and Latino) related to HIV/AIDS and other harm reduction themes. The majority of organization's funding comes from federal, state, or municipal government, i.e., from white folks. The leadership of POCC is male. The majority of the people who are served by the organization are also male.

According to conversations I've had with the parties involved, the leadership of POCC had some criticisms of the way in which Black Pride NYC, the annual event, had been organized. They had been sponsors in previous years and therefore had a certain level of access to the organizing process to make a legitimate critique. There were several unsuccessful attempts made by both the leadership of Black Pride NYC, Inc. and POCC to resolve the matters between them. They attempted an unsuccessful mediation. Eventually, POCC decided to organize a separate set of Pride events under the name Pride in the City.

I have several comments about the situation that I think are not only useful for New York but may also be instructive for people across the country. We need independent, indigenous sources of funding for social service and community-based organizations in our communities so that decisions about the kinds of services that are provided, the strategies for health maintenance, and the approaches to providing service to our communities no longer remain under the control of white folks be they in government or a large foundation. White folks can't determine appropriate public health policy for us. Our social service and community-based organizations cannot provide appropriate public health services to us while under the confines of priorities, standards, and directives of white folks. Unfortunately, if you look at the names of the larger sponsors of Black Pride events, you will see Black Pride making the same mistake. They are relying upon white folks to fund their annual events. These white folks from the corporate world also come with a set of priorities, standards, and directives that are also not in our interest.

So, essentially, Black Pride NYC, Inc. is dueling with white folks' money from the corporate world and POCC is dueling with white folks' money from government. Beyond the workshops, parties, get-togethers, and entertaining performances what long-term progressive results do we, as a community, get from these events? *We still don't have the independent sources of funding for substantial community development.*

The other question I have about this process is why were there only Black men involved in this process? Where were the Black women and Black Transgender folks? Could their presence have provided some balance to the testosterone-heavy proceedings between the two organizations? As a man I know how easy it is for us to slip into a dick-measuring contest while appearing to be just handling business. Our egos are easily bruised but we find it so difficult to say that we feel personally hurt. We are quicker to use the power of our position or the authority of our role to "take care of some silly queen who thinks she is *fab* but don't really know who she's dealing with." I've seen this dynamic play out particularly among men who are in community service work so much so that now I stay clear of groups that are supposed to be about the entire community but don't have various genders represented as full members within the leadership.

I sat in a bar with another writer who is nationally-syndicated and relatively famous. The conversation eventually led to the topic of the two Black Prides in NYC and he mentioned that he was going to write an article about it. Having read his columns before, I challenged him about how he would write the article. I feel he typically is so politically correct in his articles that I rarely find a position in his work because it so strategically avoids offending anyone. As I finished challenging him, I started to challenge myself. I had decided I wouldn't write about this because I knew the individuals involved so well. I had to confront my motivations to not offend.

I have no animosity toward any of the parties involved. I know most of them personally and consider them colleagues. But I must also challenge what I believe is the shortsightedness that goes beyond the particular individuals involved and permeates the leadership in our community in general. I hope that everyone will be able to read my perspective in the spirit in which it has been given—to contribute to the building of our communities and the building of our selves.

SCRAMBLING/FIGHTING TO SUCK FARRAKHAN'S DICK: BMX-NY AND NBJC

The October 15, 2005 Millions More Movement March brought to the surface tension between the National Black Justice Coalition and Black Men's Xchange-New York. Both groups who claim to serve Black folks pitted themselves against each other to fill the one slot for a representation of the non-heterosexual part of the Black community at the rally. I penned this article just before the event.

This weekend thousands if not millions of Black folks will answer the call of Nation of Islam's Minister Louis Farrakhan to join him on the mall in Washington DC for the Millions More Movement March (really a rally/demonstration rather than a march since people will be stationary during the event rather than moving through the city)—AKA the Million Man March Reloaded.

At some point the National Black Justice Coalition (NBJC) got involved in lobbying efforts to have "gay-identified" speakers at the march. They had been quite hopeful because Farrakhan embraced Keith Boykin at a media event Tavis Smiley organized earlier this year. Based upon that hope, they have lobbied so-called march "organizers" and they've lobbied Minister Farrakhan directly.

Rather than go with any of the NBJC-suggested candidates for the esteemed role of "honorary faggot for queer comments" (not to be confused with the special assistant to the President on LGBT affairs role that Keith held in the Clinton Administration) at the rally, Farrakhan and crew went with a leading member of the Black Men's Xchange of New York (BMX-NY), Cleo Manago. It was reported in a mainstream (read European-American) gay press outlet that this was a slap in the face to NBJC because, based upon the report, BMX-NY has been critical of organizations like the NBJC in that Cleo has questioned the ideological independence of Black gay-identified groups from white gay politics especially on issues that specifically or disproportionately affect Black folks. All of that is not my issue here. I have several other issues with what happened.

I haven't heard either group, BMX-NY or NBJC, question the legitimacy of the rally in the first place. Did they read Malcolm X's critique of the 1963 March on Washington called by A. Phillip Randolph and MLK, Jr, and organized by that hot ass, diva, faggot extraordinaire Bayard Rustin? I love Bayard for being one of a very few truly creative thinking people during his time. Did they hear the admonitions against the Million Man March, ten years ago, by brilliant, visionary elders such as John Henrik Clarke? Why seek or accept a place at a table that is problematic in the first place? Clarke criticized the MMM for bringing Black dollars into the hands of white companies that would benefit from the travel and lodging of the millions of men going to DC when those dollars could be put into a fund to build shoe companies, hotel companies, airline companies, textile companies, etc. Clarke called the MMM a "con game."

Why focus so much public attention on the rally when the follow-up and aftermath of the rally are so much more important to the mobilization of our people? How are the plans for the follow-up/aftermath in line with the interests of our communities as wholes rather than parts? That should have been the focus of any work on this thing. The question should have been raised, "Where do we want to have this thing end up? Based upon the goals, what should (if anything) happen at the rally and who should be there on stage speaking?"

Did anyone ask how this would be any different from POWER or the MMM in that Farrakhan would provide a great show—entertaining, exhilarating, and inspiring—that would eventually and definitely peter out into little to no action or major liberatory progress? Oh, you don't know what POWER is? You haven't heard of People Organized and Working for Economic Rebirth? You don't remember the NOI plan for economic empowerment in Black communities across the nation, manifested in POWER products like toiletries? Does anyone else recognize that the NOI is great at building viable structures within the very narrow context of the American Muslim Movement structure developed by Elijah Muhammad, championed by Malcolm X, and resurrected by Louis Farrakhan? But the NOI has a poor track record of being able to move the masses of Black people to do anything beyond attend Farrakhan's speaking engagements with the same enthusiasm they have when they attend a Jay-Z, 50 Cent, or Beyoncé concert.

The top-down, masculinist (male-centered, male-dominated) structure of the NOI and the thinking that surrounds the NOI is antithetical to creativity, ingenuity, and innovation. When everyone is so caught up in looking up for their directions, they don't develop the resources necessary for liberatory activity. They are too enslaved to the system to which they've attached themselves to act in ways that truly liberate themselves or their people. Why is the issue of homosexuality even worthy of discussion for an organization, NOI, which fosters such a homosocial and homoerotic environment among its male members? The Fruit of Islam (no pun intended) is a homosocial (organized around a specific gender, in this case, male culture, to the exclusion of female culture), homoerotic (centered on the beauty of one gender, in this case, Black masculinity) environment. Let's be real. Black men gravitate to the FOI to receive love from other men, men whom they deem to be strong, positive, and powerful. The training, discipline, and fraternity/ brotherhood within the FOI structure, one that seeks to control and develop the Black male body, mind, and spirit, is an erotic/sensual (of the body and soul) and I'd guess for some but not all a sexual (probably unconscious) experience. But the organization is so static and rigid in its structure, relying upon its masculinist self-image, that it can't respond to criticisms made by groups like NBJC, in authentic, creative, and substantive ways. It's no wonder a group calling its members same-gender loving was chosen. How is BMX-NY any more same-gender-loving than the FOI? How is the FOI any less?

Acceptance at the rally means nothing without critical analysis. Just because BMX-NY is more digestible to patriarchal, sexist, and heterosexist organizers because BMX-NY says they are same-gender-loving while NBJC says they are gay, there is no reason for celebration on any of our parts. If BMX-NY is going to merely change the window dressing on what people who experience same-sex desire are called, they are doing the whole of Black communities a disservice. If they are going to fall in line with the stale politics of speaking on podiums and ignore other possible roles such as maintaining the spiritual gates during an event, providing community access to ancestor spirits during an event, providing critical care during an event, providing free, health-sustaining food and nourishment during an event (not fried this and hormone-injected that), then they are making themselves into nothing more than "honorary faggots for queer comments" under the name of same-gender-loving.

PIMPS & HOS

At least as early as the late 90s, Black HIV/AIDS organizations have been "ho'ed out" by the government and other large donors. In an effort to control the quality, evaluation, and nature of HIV/AIDS education, prevention and treatment strategies and practices, funders have traditionally put restrictions on what our organizations can do to address our specific cultural needs with regard to this epidemic. Our organizations, those that have chosen to rely upon the money from the government and other large donors, have been strangled by a racist, sexist, classist, heterosexist, and erotophobic financial monopoly that has dictated what can be done and what can't, what researchers, scientists, and consultants can be hired, what strategies can be used, what can be said or not said, etc.

Organizations have been de-funded because they have stepped out of the box and gotten too creative. Our organizations have been subjected to stupid guidelines that have undermined true impact. This funding climate has cultivated a culture of stupidity, ignorance, apathy, intellectual laziness, and a dearth of creativity within our organizations. I'll give you an example. I was at a meeting of the New York State Black Gay Network, a group of professionals who work in HIV/AIDS community-based organizations for Black men. The topic of reaching Black men who have sex with men but who don't identify as gay (i.e. DL men) emerged during the discussion and these professionals— self-identified, Black gay men—were trying to figure out how their organizations could reach this population. In other words, how they could find these men and reach them with HIV/AIDS education/ information.

They struggled to identify ways to find and do outreach. This seemed pathetically hilarious to me so I said to them, "What is wrong with y'all? Why is it that when you come to work you leave all of the rest of who you are at the door to the office? You know how to reach these men. You fuck them, don't you? How do you reach them when you are trying to get some? Where do you go to find trade when you want to fuck? It's not like we don't have this information. It's that we have been so conditioned that we don't know shit or how to do this work by these white professionals who come in and tell us about who we are and what we need. Y'all sitting back waiting for the CDC to come up with a study to tell y'all how to reach the man whose dick you sucked last night."

Our organizations have been pimped by the government and the funders. They don't have the capacity to do what our communities need to address the underlying problems that we face. A ho can't save your life when his/her life is still for sale. The HIV Industrial Complex has fostered a pervasive stupidity and paralysis of analysis among those folks on the frontlines of providing HIV services and prevention interventions. People who live, fuck, and love in a particular community go into work and experience a temporary amnesia at the office door which prevents them from acknowledging that they know more about their communities than the government and funders. When they walk into work, they are forced to act as if they don't know anything about their communities not handed down by some big name researcher or the CDC.

This pandemic of ignorance in the HIV Industrial Complex has encouraged epistemological and programmatic laziness. Muscles not used for long periods of time atrophy. That's what has happened to too many directors, coordinators, and line staff in Black organizations focused on HIV prevention and case management. People in the industry have learned to not know: not know what the needs are, not know where to find the people, not know why the rates have decreased among certain groups, not know what aspects of an intervention will not work with Black folks, not know what culturally-engaging approaches look like, etc.

Though we, Black folks in public health, share a responsibility for this, we cannot hold white folks, particularly in government and funding entities, blameless. These folks, the institutional progeny of Reconstruction landowners, run plantation-like public health processes. They treat Black organizations like sharecroppers. They control the funds and therefore they dictate what is important. They know what is best for "darkie" and they let "darkie" know it at every available moment. They dole out near-subsistence funds that are allocated with little understanding of or concern for the indigenous needs and agendas of Black communities.

Like the classic pimp, the government and funders look for Black community-based organizations working on HIV to be on the streets, developing a presence in the form of street outreach teams that merely serve the interests of the government and funders. They require a return on their investment and are quick to punish a "ho who isn't acting right." Though they may flash the money and other symbols of wealth, those things never seem to trickle down to the ho. It's always the pimp who ultimately benefits from the pimp-ho relationship.

The challenge is how we, Black folks in public health, divest ourselves from our pimp-ho relationship with European-American hegemony. That will not be an easy task, to be sure. But it is one that we must do if we are to realize health in our communities. In fact, to divest ourselves will be an act of health as it expresses our willingness to be good to ourselves, to love ourselves, and to protect ourselves from those relationships that do us no good.

COMMON THEMES: THE PRISON INDUSTRIAL COMPLEX AND THE HIV INDUSTRIAL COMPLEX

For some time now, I've been thinking about the commonalities that exist between the prison industrial complex and the HIV industrial complex. For those who don't know, there's been a lot of work done by various individuals and organization on the issue of the prison industrial complex, most notably, by Critical Resistance (CR).

According to CR, the prison industrial complex (PIC) is "a complicated system situated at the intersection of governmental and private interests that uses prisons as a solution to social, political, and economic problems. The PIC depends upon the oppressive systems of racism, classism, sexism, and homophobia. It includes human rights violations, the death penalty, industry and labor issues, policing, courts, media, community powerlessness, the imprisonment of political prisoners, and the elimination of dissent."

First let me clarify what I mean by the HIV industrial complex. Borrowing from Critical Resistance's definition of the PIC, the HIV industrial complex (HIVIC) is a complicated system situated at the intersection of governmental and private interests that uses the HIV virus as: a cause of certain forms of sickness and death throughout the world; a way to problematize a number of social-sexual interactions and exercise social control; and a reason for the transfer of millions of dollars from individual taxpayers and consumers to various corporate and private interests. The HIVIC depends upon the oppressive systems of racism, classism, sexism, and heterosexism. It includes human rights violations, public health policy, social policy like abstinence only, industry and labor issues, policing, media, community powerlessness, medical ethics issues, research ethics issues, and the elimination of dissent. The HIV industrial Complex includes: Centers for Disease Control, the National Institutes of Health, pharmaceutical companies, condom companies, HIV researchers, AIDS service organizations (ASOs), community-based organizations (CBOs) focused on HIV, the World Health Organization, and other individuals and public/private entities involved. So what commonalities do I see between the prison industrial complex and the HIV industrial complex?

Disproportionate Effect Upon People of Color and Poor People

Both the Prison and HIV industrial Complexes disproportionately affect people of color, particularly African-American and Latino, and poor, working class people. The wealthy are able to use their resources to receive better treatment and care when they are in contact with these systems.

Contribution to Intra-Class Warfare

Just like poor and working class people who work as prison staff become dependent upon and economically advantaged by the warehousing of their fellow citizens in prisons, so too do poor and working class people who work as HIV prevention and education staff become dependent upon and economically advantaged by the seroconversions of their fellow citizens. What would it mean if criminal justice and HIV were "cured?" No more warehousing of people in prisons and no more need for the various prison employees and ancillary positions. No more seroconversion and no more need for ASO and CBO executive directors, community health specialists, peer educators, HIV researchers, and other people who make a living based upon the fact that people are seroconverting.

The Use of Moralism to Achieve Political Aims

The banner of "law and order" has often been used to promote, justify, and validate the criminal justice approach to marginalized, transgressive, and anti-social human behavior in the US. It has contributed to the US having the highest prison population in the World (Research, Development and Statistics Directorate of Home Office, 2003). Using Protestant and European Jewish moral codes, the "morally upright" of US society have designated various behaviors criminal and established systems for the dissemination of punishments for those who abridge these codes. The banner of "decency and health" has often been used to promote, justify, and validate the public health approach to marginalized and transgressive human behaviors in the US. Using Protestant and European Jewish moral codes, the "morally upright" have designated various behaviors unhealthy and/or risky and established systems for the surveillance and discouragement of those marginalized and transgressive human behaviors.

Vehicle for Moving Money Into the Hands of the Wealthy

The Prison and the HIV Industrial Complexes have provided a means for the transfer of millions of dollars from taxpayers and consumers to prison construction companies, prison management companies, pharmaceutical companies, research institutions, and scientists. People are becoming very wealthy from the imprisonment of fellow citizens and the seroconversions of fellow citizens.

AUTHENTICALLY ASSESSING PUBLIC HEALTH'S RESPONSE TO HIV

Part of the problem with early public health messages concerning HIV and AIDS was that they identified groups rather than behaviors as high-risk. That policy and practice were manifestations of heterosexism and racism. Remember when HIV/AIDS was primarily associated with Haitians and Africans. What should have been said and what should be said now is that there are several high-risk behaviors that can expose one to HIV infection: (1) condomless anal sex; (2) condomless vaginal sex; and (3) use of used needles. If that was the public health message in the early days of the epidemic, I think that people who identify as heterosexual and people whose sexual practice is primarily heterosexual would have taken a more responsible, more empowered, and more accountable approach to their sexual decision making.

Instead, the public health community gave heterosexually active folks a pass on having to directly confront the health consequences of their sexual practices. Men who have sex with men exclusively/primarily have had their sexual lives devastated by HIV education/prevention. Noted Black gay literary figure Essex Hemphill once wrote, "Now we think as we fuck, this nut might kill us." For decades, Black men who have sex with men had their sexual pleasure interrupted by thoughts of disease and death. But that's the reality with which many of us have lived.

Now many heterosexual-defined women and men have to do the same thing. Welcome to the club. Now that heterosexually-identified folks are beginning to see that we are all one and we are not just our brother's/sister's keeper we are our brother/sister maybe we can solve these problems together—like we should have been doing in the first place.

My critique isn't based upon a desire to ignore and/or minimize the seriousness of the seroconversion rates of my sisters and brothers. In fact, it's because of my commitment to the health and healing of my sisters and brothers that I am enraged by the way people have been exploiting and capitalizing on our pain and suffering and distracting us from creating real systems of health and healing within our communities.

Personal responsibility is important for all of us. And I would add to that sexual empowerment and sexual agency. One of the reasons why I created Black Funk was to contribute to the development of power and agency in the sexual lives of people of color. The sister who does not feel empowered to decide that a condom will be used because of her perception of him as a "straight" man is to me similar to the brother who does not feel empowered to be sensual (non-sexual) with another man for fear of losing his perceived sexual identity.

The way the CDC, the media, HIV CBOs, et al have fetishized Black men who have sex with men as well as have sex women but who don't use the "approved" sexual identity vocabulary is almost to the level of a parasitic, voyeuristic pornography. People are trying to get off financially (in terms of viewership/readership with the media, grants and contracts with HIV CBOs, and federal spending with the CDC) and socially (in terms of more social policies giving greater control to power elites to control, manipulate, and exploit sexuality) on the sex that this group out there, "DL" Black men, is having.

The CDC, the media, HIV CBOs, et al will argue that their interest is the safety of folks. Safety is an overly used word. Black people in this country are not safe, have never been safe, and will not be safe as long as the current systems and structures of power persist. As a Black person, you wake up in the morning and your ass is on the line. So we need to get away from this false notion of safety and talk about what will really make things safe for us here. We need to question ourselves about the degree to which we are willing to take responsible action for our freedom and that doesn't mean slipping on a condom or telling your women you like dick up your ass or down your throat. That means community building, consciousness raising, economic development, healing, transformation, and redesigning power in this country and in the world.

When I talk about the sexual identity categories I'm not talking about them as merely theoretical concepts. They have currency in all of our lives and people are making fucked up decisions in not accessing their sexual power because of their wholesale consumption of these terms. One of my hopes is that people will stop applying the terms altogether in relation to identity. There are no "gay, straight, or bisexual" people, only "gay, straight, and bisexual" preferences, behaviors, feelings, desires, and sexual activities.

I believe that sister who has had sex with men exclusively who is able to drop the straight label in referring to herself is more likely to not place the straight label, and all the accompanying assumptions, on the male partners she encounters. Part of the issue in this situation is that both men and women have been socialized to expect certain behaviors from men that are associated with what it means to be a man in this society. Men of color are burdened by the pressures to fulfill the assumptions within our communities of what men are supposed to be despite the many obstacles socially engineered to prevent us from achieving manhood. Whether it is the thug/b-boy, the corporate brother, the pimp/hustler, or the angry Black man, popular configurations of Black manhood are problematic.

I am frustrated by the media and government's (re)presentation of the issues because they have set up such polarizing dynamics in our communities. For many men who have sex with men, the issue of HIV/AIDS is something we live with everyday. When we have a blemish we didn't notice before, a cold that has appeared out of season and that lingers a bit too long, a sudden feeling of lethargy, a condom that breaks during sex, or a sexual exchange with someone we haven't known for long, we confront the specter of HIV and AIDS. For us HIV/AIDS is everywhere and is an integral part of our lives. We've had friends, lovers, mentors, and mentees die as a result.

Every time I've visited a friend in the hospital who was HIV+ I not only had to deal with the possibility of his death but also the potentiality of my own. For those of you who don't know this reality, try to understand what that's like and the impact of having that experience over and over and over again. I'm sharing this to say to you that as a Black man who has had sex with men and women, who has been touched by the impact of HIV/AIDS personally, who worked in the late 90s massaging, washing the feet of, and caring for people living with HIV/AIDS, the conversation about DL minimizes, ignores, and devalues the immense pain and suffering that I've experienced because of this disease as well as the way it has been addressed in this society. The DL conversation minimizes, ignores, and devalues, the immense pain, suffering, and social costs that I've experienced because I've chosen to affirm my sexuality publicly.

Those of us who live in the community live with HIV and AIDS even when we are HIV negative. We have been at the forefront of caring for, loving, and supporting people who have tested positive for HIV. One issue that I had with the Oprah episode about the DL was that she, Oprah, made this grand statement at the beginning of the show about how important this issue was for her as a Black woman and how alarmed she was. Beyond hosting a show about the topic, she did nothing to demonstrate the importance and alarm represented in her comments during the show. What would it have meant for Black women, HIV/AIDS organizations, and the public health community if, at the end of the show, Oprah had pledged 5 million dollars over the course of 5 years to the creation of or support of an HIV/AIDS organization dedicated specifically to Black women's issues/needs in the city of Chicago or 100 million dollars over the course of 10 years to the creation of or support of an HIV/AIDS organization dedicated specifically to Black women's issues/needs in the US? That, to me, would have indicated a real sense of alarm and commitment by the billionairess.

Since 2004 in various media sources, Black men who have covert sex with men and women, also known in those sources as men on the DL, have been portrayed as the single greatest means for Black women to contract the life threatening health condition, HIV/AIDS. It was on

Oprah, in the New York Times, on web sites, and in books; it seemed as though everyone was talking about it.

Along comes the discovery of Gential HPV Infection and the human papillomavirus and we witness a very interesting difference in social policy and cultural practice. Gential HPV infection is a sexually transmitted infection that, very recently, has been causally linked to cervical cancer. Genital HPV infection, an "incurable" sexually transmitted infection, was linked to a disease that the American Cancer Association estimated would kill 3700 women in the United States by the end of 2006. There was no scapegoating of specific individuals. There was no outcry from those same media sources that raised the alarmist flag. No one put out the message "Heterosexual/Straight men are the cause of cervical cancer among women." Why? Because racism, sexism, and heterosexism play important roles in how public health is managed in the United States.

It is very painful to hear people talk—about your life and the lives of those you have loved who have died—with no real understanding of what they are talking about and with only a set of statistics, sensationalized stories, and "experts" who are financially benefiting from the deaths of your loved ones. I am not an advocate for unsafe sexual behavior or unsafe sexual culture. Nor am I an advocate for taking actions that expose people to probable harm. I don't have to be an advocate for those things. People are doing those things without regard for my opinions or advocacy. At the same time, I've realized that we live in a society that has necessarily made sexual expression unsafe.

There is little in the way of culturally-competent, politically conscious, comprehensive sexual education in this country. People are running around filled with ignorance, misinformation, religiously and culturally motivated biases, prejudices, preferences—that have little to do with authentic desire, pleasure, and passion—and political agendas that are more about the control of political, economic, and sexual resources, rather than authentic cultivation of the human spirit.

A DAY AT THE FREE CLINIC

I spent a day at a local free clinic run by New York City's Department of Health and Mental Hygiene to get tested for HIV, gonorrhea, syphilis, chlamydia, and whatever else gets tested at these places. Here's the story of the adventure.

I walk into the large brick building reminiscent of structures of the 1940s—industrial revolution meets wartime functionalism. I feel the weight of bureaucracy settle onto my shoulders as I ride the metal tomb of an elevator up to the floor that plays host to the testing center.

As the doors of the elevator open, a wall painted with a mixture of what appears to be benign neglect, autocratic convenience, stale utilitarianism, and pee confronts me. "Where the fuck do I go from here?" I ask myself since there are no markers for where to go next. The security guard downstairs, already busy helping to redirect someone to another facility for pediatric issues, did not bother to do more than to confirm the floor that I already knew the clinic to be on. I haven't even received one test result yet and already I feel lost, afraid, intimidated, and alone.

I walk off the elevator and discover a group of "waiters" scattered in seats in an area to my right. I assume that I'm expected to join them. Their gazes—making sure they don't know me, making sure I don't know them—and their facial expressions tell me they are also here to get tested. I don't feel I can ask them if this is the right place or who I should see to sign in. I don't want to break the anonymity that we all are so desperately trying to maintain. We don't want to break the alienation we've built up in the ride in the elevator. To do so would be to confront the humanity of our lives—we have desires, emotions, feelings for other human beings; we have sex with these human beings we desire, love, feel for; and we have fears and concerns about our health as a result of those loves and desires. But there's also a specificity to our humanity that's equally present—we don't have health insurance; many of us are poor or the working poor. Our access to the nice, clean offices of a private doctor is limited.

There are various kinds of bodies that inhabit the seats. Most are Black or Latino though there are a few that are not. There are males and females, no trannies. There's a Latino family—mother, father, and four children. A cute Caribbean couple—two men, one in business casual, the other in hip hop cool. I pray they avoid the B-boy blues of a positive test result and I marvel at the expression of love, conscientiousness, and routine in their relationship—they get tested together. That's so 21st Century American Gothic.

I sit among my fellow public health citizens. The design of the room has us all seated facing a wall a few feet away. Is this some architectural metaphor for the system's forecast for us—all headed in the same direction, hitting a wall? Mounted on that wall is a television obviously connected to a VCR hidden somewhere in the nether regions of the office. Snow and graining noise pours out the black box filling the room with white noise's irritating cousin, static. Someone must have hit the play button because a video abruptly begins on the screen.

This video was obviously made as the HIV equivalent to "Scared Straight." The video uses real people to tell their HIV stories in the hope of influencing the sexual decision-making of those of us sitting in the room watching it. But the video was made in the 80s. You can tell because of the way the people are dressed, their hairstyles, and the degree to which their bodies have been ravaged by drugs, disease, and economic oppression. And I thought the metaphor of all of us hitting the wall was bad. Now we're subjected to face a future of HIV's past displayed on the video.

I'm already terrified about this test and the impact the results will have on my life. Regardless of whether there's a significant reason for concern, getting an HIV test always quickens the blood and creates much anxiety. You don't have to have done anything. It's an irrational fear promulgated by the socially induced paranoia of decades of HIV prevention propaganda.

I sit here at the juncture of every HIV prevention message I received since high school and my memory of every sexual act I've engaged in since first receiving those messages. I'm trying to hold it together, not appear as terrified as I am and now I'm confronted by this ghost of the past, "HIV=DEATH," in the guise of a video. I wonder whose brainchild it is to play this video long after its dubious truth has any connection to current reality. Is it a disaffected, thoughtless bureaucrat who just follows the mandate to provide prevention messages while clients wait? Or is it a religiously inspired, dogma-supported bureaucrat with a complex mix of pity, disgust, and condescension who plays the tape to scare these sinners into living a healthier=more righteous=more God-fearing life? Whatever the reason and whoever the person responsible, to me, the decision to play this video at this time in this place was a colossal mistake, and a breakdown in human empathy.

Finally, they call me in to the doctor, a 50-ish, short, pink-skinned man. He takes a brief and inadequate sexual history. He asks me about my sexual history with women. I wait for his questions about my sexual history with men. They never come. He moves on to take the samples he needs for the tests. He gives me a date to return and I'm out. But wait, where are the questions about my sexual history with men? Why doesn't he ask me about that? Is it because I present as masculine and therefore such questions are unwarranted in his mind? Masculine equals heterosexual, right? Sex with women equals heterosexual, right?

I walked into this clinic to get tested for sexually transmitted diseases and unintentionally walked into a test of the public health system's capacity to adequately respond to the sexual realities of the public for whom they serve.

WHOSE BOOTY IS THIS?
BAREBACKING, ADVOCACY,
AND THE RIGHT TO FUCK

A European-American writer from The Advocate *wrote an article on this topic not long after I wrote this article, a version of which originally appeared in the program guide for Pride In the City, an annual festival for Black LGBT/Q/SGL/Same-Sex Attracted people in New York City. Without referencing my article or seeking to interview me and dismissing the comments of other HIV prevention professionals whose views were contrary to the agenda of the author, the author wrote an attack piece which re-states and replays clichéd images of Black and Latino men. Readers were again transported into a dark and seedy underworld where lascivious Black and Latino men engage in savage, hedonistic, unscrupulous debauchery all through the lens of the Euro-American adventurer/reporter and his Euro-American-identified native key informants.*

The Advocate *demonstrates its Eurocentricism and white supremacy by positioning a Euro-American reporter to tell the world and us about what Black and Latino men "reportedly" do. The reasons why any of the individuals involved in the story would collaborate with this new millennium safari—under the guise of public health and keeping our brothers safe—has been discussed by various authors e.g., Frantz Fanon's "Black Skin, White Masks," Albert Memmi's "The Colonizer and The Colonized," and E. Franklin Frazier's "Black Bourgeoisie." We continue to ally ourselves with folks who don't have our best interests at heart and who unconsciously/consciously seek to exploit our communities for their gain. Too many of us continue to ignore the fact that the master's tools won't dismantle the master's house.*

It would have taken the writer five minutes to do his homework prior to writing the story and look up books such as "Policing Public Sex" or Eric Rofes' "Reviving the Tribe" and "Dry Bones Breathe" to inform himself of the critical issues at play for men who practice same-sex desire from various cultural communities in the United States.

All in all, this was truly a poor attempt at journalism and a great example of cultural ignorance and arrogance by the Euro-American reporter Sean Kennedy.

In the spring of 2006, a unique thing happened. A community-based organization (CBO), committed "to improving the quality of life within the New York City Black gay community by effectively fighting the triple threat of AIDS, homophobia and racism through education, advocacy, health and wellness and social support" decided to launch a picket of a sex party in Harlem that catered to Black and Latino men. To my knowledge, the decision was unprecedented for a Black organization in the 25-year history of HIV. The nature of the sex party was also significant in that the party was promoted as a "raw" sex party in which "anyone caught using jimmies [condoms] will be asked to leave with no refund given!!!" The CBO called on concerned members of the community to join them in picketing outside of the apartment building where the party was hosted. In response to the potential of a picket, the party promoters canceled the party for the weekend of the picket.

This incident represents an important moment in our (his)story as Black men who experience same-sex desire. If we take a closer look at it, reflecting on the underlying messages, competing/coalescing priorities and principles, and the clashing/collapsing of worldviews, the incident has the potential to tell us a lot about who we are, who we've become, and where we may be headed as members of the various tribes of men thrown together into this stew called Black gay community. Of course at the center of this discussion must also be a focus on who we fuck, why we fuck, and how we fuck.

"Raw" sex, which when referring to anal sex between men is also called barebacking, intentional, condomless, anal intercourse, and a host of other terms, has been made troubling, problematic, dangerous, and irresponsible by the same mechanism that has historically made sex between men in any form troubling, problematic, dangerous, irresponsible, etc. That mechanism can be termed sexism-heterosexism, the combination of forces that makes women-bad, men-good, queer-bad, and straight-good. Raw sex between men was no more illegitimate than any other sex between men until the force of sexism-heterosexism made it so. Likewise, in the context of sex between men, using condoms has been no more legitimate than sex without condoms until sexism-heterosexism made it so. HIV/AIDS serves as a justifying agent that has legitimized the entrance of the coercive force of the government, through the vehicle of the state-function we call public health, into our bedrooms, cruising spaces, public sex venues, and sex parties.

Our sex lives as men of color who experience same-sex desire have become issues of national security, thereby labeling us *de facto* sexual terrorists, the Rahiems, Jamals, Hectors, Tyrones, and Anthonys, on the national terrorist watch list alongside the Osama. So what does it mean when *our* organizations perform raids on *our* sexual spaces using the same language and imagery of the State and under the banner of "keeping us safe?" Why wasn't another part of the raw sex party's policy, "must be in-shape/toned/muscular...No fats or big guts," considered equally if not more problematic to the well-being, health, and vitality of our communities? Maybe, the policing of acceptable body forms can't be considered homophobic but it does appear heterophobic (as in fear of difference), self-hatred, and an attack on the vitality in diversity within groups; and that too equals death.

As a collection of communities, we have been socialized to recoil at the notion of condomless anal sex while not flinching at the expression of hatred from within those communities toward certain types of bodies (e.g., fat bodies and big guts) and certain forms of gender expression (e.g., effeminacy and fem bois/men). We have been conditioned to believe that the preference for condomless sex is socially irresponsible and injurious to the community while the preference for and insistence upon "in-shape/toned/muscular," straight-acting, masculine, thug bodies is just a matter of personal choice and freedom beyond criticism, interrogation, or critical reflection.

Little thought is given to the relationship between both preferences. How often do we question the degree to which our preference for condomless anal sex is influenced by our preference for "in-shape/toned/muscular" bodies? Whom do we choose to bareback with and do those partners share similar body characteristics or gender characteristics? If so, why? Is it because we have chosen to believe that an "in-shape/toned/muscular" body is a "healthy" body, a masculine disposition is a "healthy" disposition, absent of disease or infection? Is it because we feel honored to have been selected by someone with an "in-shape/toned/muscular" body or a "masculine" disposition to be a sexual partner and therefore obligated to have sex the way we believe they want it (i.e., without a condom) or compelled to receive their "valuable/valued" seed in our "less than valuable/valued" bodies?

In choosing this party as a target, with its explicit no condom policy, was not the organization unintentionally, uncritically yet indirectly promoting the idea that sex without condoms isn't happening in the dark, oftentimes pitch black, fuck rooms of the "safer sex" parties where condoms are available (when you can find them in the dark)? I am not indicting anyone. I am merely suggesting that here is a moment to consider what our avenues to liberation, empowerment, and action are; what the consequences to our use and abuse of those avenues are.

I will end by taking this moment to say, with the same feeling of naturalness, privilege, and entitlement that people who identify as straight or heterosexual would, "I love fucking without condoms and do so every opportunity that I can." Now, ask me how I do it and you might learn something.

Sexuality

LIBERATION OR MURDER:
WAYS WE RESPOND TO
ECSTASY & PLEASURES

There are moments, encounters that expose and initiate us to a new sexual something that had been, up to that point, beyond our conscious awareness or sensual vocabulary. Some of those moments are fairly common, a first kiss. Others of them are common to a subset of us:

- Our first wet dream,
- Our first sexual encounter,
- Our first sexual encounter with someone of the same sex,
- Our first sexual encounter with/as a trannie,

- Our first anal sex experience (giving, receiving, same-sex, or opposite-sex),
- Our first oral sex experience,
- Our first orgasm,
- Our first time tasting cum, piss, blood, or shit as a sexual act,
- Our first time using restraints during sex,
- Our first time having sex without a condom,
- Our first threesome or group scene, or
- Our first time having sex outside, etc.

In those moments, our bodies-minds-spirits have an opportunity to learn a new vocabulary of pleasure, sensuality, and the erotic. A new reality is revealed and recorded in our cells and we are forever changed. We move, think, and feel differently. We are challenged to confront the limitations of our previous perception of the world and incorporate this new knowing. The old way can't survive unchanged. It must adapt or die to this new reality that has been made manifest.

Such a requirement for change can be very threatening on a personal and a social level. To disrupt, confound, or even shatter the old knowing on either the personal or social level may rub up against deeply rooted needs or interests such as needs for order, predictability, or control. How can we maintain the status quo if we allow something so powerful, so enrapturing, so primal a place in our world? It's too frightening a possibility and yet by the time we try to figure out how to quash "it" it is too late because we're already in the moment feeling what we're feeling, going through it.

It takes even more energy, a force of greater magnitude, to quash the pressure to change in response to the new knowing. That's why we hear stories of people, unwilling to accommodate the new reality, going into a rage after such an experience, becoming violent, even killing the other person (who is perceived as the catalyst of the erotic energy) or themselves (the site of the erotic energy) to silence the voice of change. It's cosmically profound that we call upon rage to extinguish passion in the face of our fear. Said another way, when we are frightened by the experience of a threatening and unfamiliar passion, too many of us use rage as a way out rather than dealing with the difficulty of adjusting to the new learning.

There is liberation in this new learning. These moments open our eyes to the walls that have been constructed to constrain our pleasures, desires, passions, and bodies. Once aware of the walls, we're better able to climb over them, break through them, walk around them, or tunnel under them. We can choose to draw power from these moments in service to our growth and liberation. We can choose to make these moments moments of erotic agitation in the struggle for our sensual empowerment. The choice is ours on a personal and a social level. We can choose liberation or murder in the face of ecstasy in the ways we respond to new pleasures we encounter along our life journey.

What do you choose?

ON BEING A CELIBATE, SEX RADICAL

In the fall of 2005, I made the decision to practice celibacy for the foreseeable future. As a 33-year old, HIV negative, bisexually-active man of African ancestry, I had had a lot of sex since the age of 21—a lot of, what some might consider, great sex. At the point that I had very nearly completed a powerful PhD program and seeing the dawning of a promising career as a research scientist and a rewarding (spiritually, financially, emotionally) career as a sex educator, I was tired of being unsatisfied, unfulfilled in my relationships with brothers. I was tired of making relationship choices (who I choose, why I choose them) that didn't garner, couldn't garner, the intimacy, commitment, and fulfillment I desired.

I really valued intimacy and the erotic. Audre Lorde said the erotic was "those physical, emotional, and psychic expressions of what is deepest and strongest and richest within each of us, being shared: the passion of love, in its deepest meanings." Too few of the men that I met and found attractive possessed the capacity for sharing the erotic. No, it was not about me just wanting "bad boys." That's a stale story that too easily explained something more complex. There were no good boys or bad boys. No good women or chicken heads. There were only other people like me trying to make it in the world with the skills and resources they had.

I understood that where we each are in our processes could change over time. And while I appreciated the fact that everyone is going through their own process, I also didn't have to submit myself, or subject myself to someone else's process especially when that process didn't affirm the values that I was attempting to uplift in my life. I'd done that already, too many times. So, I did something different. In a sexual climate in which sex waits perched in the next moment while connectedness is as invisible and elusive as air, my decision to be celibate and value sex, intimacy, the erotic, and emotional fulfillment was a declaration of optimism. I believed in passionate sex, intimacy, the erotic, and emotional fulfillment so much that I was willing to refuse anything less so that I would fully embrace them when they showed themselves.

My celibacy was a success. During the period of five weeks, I was able to clarify and integrate my internal world. The following paragraphs are my journal entries from that period. I wrote the journal as a part of my column, *From the Cave*, on www.blackfunk.org. It was a way to communicate my experiences during the celibacy and engage readers in a conversation about the nature of sexual relations.

The Celibacy Chronicles: Week Two

So tomorrow will make a week of celibacy for me. What does that mean? Well, it means that it will be a week since I made the decision to not have sex outside of the context of an intimate, committed, fulfilling, and long-tern relationship with a man—no more engaging in sex with men or women with whom I can't share intimacy, vulnerability, and connectedness during sex or after sex.

It's been an interesting week. I found that the things that I wasn't taking care of before last week, things that I could have said I wasn't taking care of because of my active sex life, I still didn't take care of. There goes the theory that sex was deterring me from getting certain things accomplished in my life. I definitely have shit that I need to get done, some of that connected with the list of "Heru's activities," that I haven't done and don't do in a timely manner. So one week of no sex later, and those things still aren't done. I'll get to them though.

How do you tell people who want to have sex with you that you're celibate? For people whom I've had sex with multiple times, it's been somewhat awkward, for me at least. I guess because of my reasons for practicing celibacy. Sharing those reasons with people with whom I've had sex on multiple occasions sounds like a judgment to me about them or about my relationship with them. It's like saying, "Well, I'm not having sex right now because you're not what I want and you couldn't give me what I want so I'm holding out for what I want." And that's not what I intended my celibacy to be about nor what I want to be communicated to them. My celibacy isn't about past or current relationships. It's about me and about future relationships. Is it about past relationships too?

Anyway, those conversations have been awkward. One brother who I dated for several months before he had to move back down South told me that I needed to stop wasting time with brothers in New York and to move down there with him. Talking via phone, he really stepped to me on some Billy Dee Williams in *Mahogany* shit that kind of fucked me up because I've always been the Billy Dee in the relationship to his Diana Ross. He came with the "you know if you move down here with me you'd be with someone who loves you, who knows how to treat you, who can build a life with you." Damn. I told him I'd seriously consider it. Right now, contractual and professional obligations prevent me from leaving New York prior to June of next year.

A sister with whom I've had an on-again, off-again sexual relationship told me I should have told her prior to making my decision so she could have gotten a little something in before I made my decision. What does it mean that I have chosen to participate in the often problematic sexual politics between men when there's a woman—actually, a couple of women—that I could engage in a relationship, who have the capacity to be intimate, committed, vulnerable, etc?

I could most definitely be in a relationship with a woman but that relationship couldn't be monogamous. While I can be emotionally and sexually connected to a woman, there are emotional and sexual parts of me that have not been sufficiently fed by a woman. Men feed those parts of me, however briefly.

Today, while I was on the train reading Samuel R. Delany's autobiography, *The Motion of Light in Water: Sex and Science Fiction Writing in the East Village*, (around pps. 400-480) I began the process of healing from my ex's and my ex-best friend's decision to get together after my ex and I split. Even though I ended the relationship with her, a relationship that lasted 10 years, I was so hurt by their decision to get together. I've had dreams/nightmares about it for the last year off and on. While I was reading Delany's description of a relationship he, his wife, and another man had many years ago, I realized the source of my pain. I was hurt that he, my former best friend, hadn't chosen to be with both of us as lovers. In the face of the breech (the ending of the relationship) between her and I, he hadn't decided to try to be the bridge between us. And there was definitely room for him too. He had lived with us for a time years ago. He was obviously attracted to her. His attraction toward me was more complex, filled with all the usual portions of homophobia, body fascism, jealousy, curiosity, and passivity indicative of a self-defined straight dude who had been molested as a frail, dark skinned kid. He grew to become a quick-witted, buffed, semi-attractive man with a reputation for carrying a big dick and a mean stroke.

I realize now that there was no way that he was going to approach me directly, no way he was going to be intimate and vulnerable in the way that I need for a man to be for me to engage him. His intimacy and vulnerability came in other, somewhat conflicted forms. Like when he, with a pulled muscle in his back, stood nude in the shower, back and ass to me, while I massaged him and let the warm water fall on the affected shoulder.

He was another brother in my life capable of moments of physical intimacy and vulnerability when it served his needs—who could not extend the intimacy and vulnerability beyond a servicing of his needs. On the train today, reading about Delany's experience, I connected with my desire for the relationship that the three of us shared to have been more than it was and my hurt at the fact that they went ahead with the relationship after I left. That's what was painful for me, even though I could no longer support the weight of the demands of the relationship with her. With the realization came a feeling of goodwill toward the two of them—I hope they are good to each other; I hope they give each other what they need. And I no longer need to or want to be a part of it.

We had an exhibition of my godson Charly's work at Black Funk. The exhibition was great. It was really powerfully beautiful and a number of times during the evening I started to tear up because the beauty of the environment was penetrating every pore of my body so much that I felt overwhelmed.

One of the things that moment brought up—related to my being celibate—was how the spiritual/energetic environment of Black Funk makes people horny. Spending so much time in the space, I forget how much and how the space affects people. I've heard people saying on countless occasions how the space makes them horny or it opens them up. Oftentimes, people will just say what a great space it is or how they really feel at peace there. But again, because I live in that space I forget what it does to people. Yet, it hasn't made being celibate difficult for me. If anything, I think it's been helpful because of the nature of the effect that the space has. It's not that Black Funk makes you want to fuck. The wanting to fuck is a secondary effect. Black Funk makes you want to connect, to bridge gaps, to be intimate, to be erotic in the Lordean sense of the word. People often translate that into wanting to fuck, wanting to have sex. But really that's just a translation of a different calling.

I think my choice to be celibate allowed me to see more distinctly and clearly that underlying effect. Having that recognition, I'm even more committed to not having sex without connection, commitment, intimacy, and love rather than less committed. If there is any challenge to my celibacy that I see, it's the dynamic between my godson and I. Women who occupy the same space for a period of time experience their menstrual cycles converging around the same dates. Similarly, I believe that butch queens that occupy the same space for a period of time try to match each other's level of sexual activity. There convergences tend to encourage an increase rather than decrease of their individual sexual activity in an attempt to match each other. So with me being celibate and my godson not, the challenge is for me to maintain my level of sexual activity at zero in the face of his sexual activity at what it is.

Anyway, that's been the last week.

The Celibacy Chronicles: Week Three

"Are you going to masturbate?" "Does your celibacy include women?" "So does that mean that I can come over to your house, strip down nude, and walk around your place without worrying that anything is gonna happen?" "Does your celibacy mean that you won't be having sex with your leather sons?" "Have you been tempted?" People have had so many questions about my celibacy, questions I hadn't asked myself, some questions I didn't need to ask myself.

This second week has been interesting. I've noticed that my sex drive (legendary in some circles) has dissipated considerably. Faced with some very physically attractive men in my comings and goings, I haven't had a desire to have sex. Somehow, internally, sexual desire has been tied to an erotic desire (intimacy, emotional connectedness) in such a way as I don't feel sexually aroused in the absence of intimacy and emotional connectedness. That doesn't mean I haven't been sexually aroused at all. I've actually had several significant arousals. And it's telling how they've been manifesting. They are with the three people with whom I've had history. There's the sister I see from time to time that I've been desiring this week. My ex in Atlanta is another source of arousal. And my ex in North Carolina is yet another.

One of the things I decided this past week was that I was going to have sex with people with whom I shared an intimacy and emotional connection. I decided that my celibacy was going to be based in an abstinence from sex without intimacy/emotional connection. Each of these three, the sister and the two brothers (my exes), are people with whom I share an intimacy and an emotional connectedness. Each of those relationships is complicated in different ways that I won't go into now.

It's a time of great possibilities in my life and the celibacy/abstinence has played a role. My celibacy/abstinence has meant that I no longer need sex to be or use sex as the first language that I speak when I meet someone. By taking sex off the table in my initial interactions with folks, I'm asking myself new questions. I'm stepping out of previously automated practices and finding new practices, new ways of being, and new possibilities in how to be and what to do in those moments. That doesn't mean that I'm withdrawing from sex. I plan on having sex, at some point. But it does mean that I'm re-inventing the role sex has in my social life and valuing more deeply the role sex has in my intimate life.

The Celibacy Chronicles: Week Four

Everyone keeps asking me, "Have you had sex yet?" No, damn it! Stop asking me! It's like being an alcoholic in recovery being asked each day, "Have you had a drink, yet?"

Major Insights of the Past Week:

1. Fucking isn't everything. Fucking is everything. Fucking is nothing.
2. Women smell celibacy on a man and it makes them hot.
3. Men are more invested/interested in talking about what they can't get from you than what they can't offer you.
4. When sex is off the table, the barrenness of what people bring to the table is much more apparent.
5. Celibacy isn't about removing sex from your life. Celibacy is about putting life back into your sex.

The Celibacy Chronicles: Week Five and Beyond

Well it's been a while since I updated the chronicles. That's mainly been due to work and school obligations. A lot has happened since. At the end of week five, I broke my celibacy with a brother that I was feeling. He and I have seen each other, non-sexually, off and on since. It's been really challenging to engage in meaningful interaction over and on top of all the toxic shit one picks up throughout one's dating life.

I've decided to entertain cycles of celibacy and sexual activity from now on. I function better in my non-sexual life when I'm having sex. I noticed that my skin started to develop acne. My energy level and drive were constricted. And I was not a happy camper at times. I recognize that these are typical signs of "withdrawal" and that I may have, had I continued, reached another period of ease and flow with the celibacy, but my goal was not to get comfortable with celibacy. It was to use celibacy as a way of setting the stage for a new kind of relationship for myself.

Too much sexual contact though, meaning numerous sexual occasions that are not really hitting the spot, is also not productive to my healthy functioning. So I believe that the cyclical approach will be useful. Though a friend/ex-lover likened it to the bingeing and purging of bulimia, I believe that my exploration of a cyclical approach to sexual activity is consistent with my commitment to sexual exploration—learning from my sexual experiences to develop greater insight, consciousness, and empowerment in my life.

Another powerful set of occurrences that has taken place is that I've had really productive clarifying conversations with the one woman and two men that I mentioned in earlier chronicles. These conversations have provided richer perspectives on the nature and limitations of those relationships. Though the relationships have not been perfected through my practice of celibacy, they have featured a greater level of authenticity.

10-STEP PUBLIC HEALTH SEX: A RATIONAL, SOCIALLY RESPONSIBLE APPROACH TO FUCKING DEVOID OF EMOTION, PASSION, AND DESIRE

Step 1:   Recruit a potentially eligible candidate from a designated population

Step 2:   Isolate yourself and the recruit in an environment free from pathogens, viruses, or other virulent organisms

Step 3:   Simultaneously test yourself and the recruit for all known sexually transmitted infections and get hepatitis vaccinations for you and the recruit

Step 4:   Retest yourself and the recruit after 6 months

Step 5:   Administer a sexual history questionnaire to yourself and the recruit

Step 6: Review responses to the sexual history questionnaire and the results of both sexually transmitted infections tests with the recruit

Step 7: Based upon the discussion with the recruit make a rational decision about whether to engage in any form of sexual contact with the recruit

Step 8: Should you decide to engage in sexual contact with the recruit acquire the following: condoms (male and/or female depending upon your sex and the sex of your recruit), lubricant (without nonoxynol-9), and dental dams

Step 9: Participate in a training class with the recruit to learn the proper application, use, and disposal of each of the items listed in Step 8

Step 10: Engage in sexual activity with the recruit once all hepatitis vaccinations have been administered and a blood test taken to confirm the appropriate level of protection in you and your recruit has been conducted

Orgasm is optional

SLEEPING WITH THE ENEMY

One of the more painful lessons that I've learned as a person involved in this thing we call love is the lesson of sleeping with the enemy. Sleeping with the enemy is a powerfully destructive force where love is concerned. It undermines our ability to experience, enjoy, or value love in our life. It robs us of our capacity to know love when we see it and respond to love when we receive it. So what is sleeping with the enemy? Well, it may not be what you expected. Let me explain.

Ask yourself the question: How many times have you entered into a love relationship truly believing that you deserved the love you were receiving? When we don't believe that we deserve love, the person who is giving us that love becomes suspect. We begin to ask ourselves: Why is s/he with me? What does s/he really hope to get out of this? What's her/his angle?

Suspicion and contempt fester as this person who has become a mirror for our own self-contempt and loathing unconsciously frustrates us. How dare you love me with all these flaws and inadequacies? How dare you think that I'm beautiful, attractive, desirable, and worthy of love? Some of you may deny having experienced these feelings. I suggest before dismissing the phenomenon that you think about those relationships in which you manifested "insane jealousy," "pointless arguments," and "unnecessary suspicion." To what degree were these manifestations expressions of the phenomenon to which I'm referring?

When we don't believe we are worthy of love, the love we receive feels stale, sometimes corrosive. It makes us gag and choke as it sits within our throat like so much bile. It has nothing to do with how successful we are professionally or how great our bodies look or how stunning our faces look or how much money we have or how *fab* our clothes are. As long as we don't feel worthy, the external realities will still be drawn into the self-hate. We see examples around us: the person who seems to have it all together continues to find people who appear to be great matches only to go from failed relationship to failed relationship.

As a part of my ongoing self-care, I am called to ask myself how ready I am to receive the love that exists in my life, the love that is just around the corner, or the love that, although hidden from my view now, will be mine in the future. Most of us "overachievers" walk with this feeling of not being enough, not being worthy. That's why we work so hard at achieving so much, acquiring so much in an effort to one day be enough, to be worthy of love.

What is it like to be in a relationship with someone like this? Pure hell. What do you do when your love is an instigator of contempt and suspicion in your relationship? What do you do when it appears that you don't satisfy your lover's desire for abuse? Well, of course, you leave. But for those of us who haven't gotten to that point of recognizing the situation for what it is, the time spent learning those hard lessons can be painful and filled with self-doubt. Is it me or is it the more I love her/him the more s/he seems to have a problem?

Being in a relationship with someone like this can drive you insane. You're constantly on guard with your love. For those of us who want to love freely, this kind of relationship undermines that possibility. We leave these relationships sometimes asking ourselves months afterward,

"What the hell was the problem? Why couldn't things work?"

Sleeping with the Enemy can be painful and spiritually depleting. When you're not ready to really receive the love that is available to you, you can make an enemy out of those who want to share love with you. Likewise, when you've been made out to be the enemy because you love someone who is not ready to be loved, you can unwittingly get caught up in a war that you can't win—a war with no victors, only casualties.

WHEN LOVE ISN'T ENOUGH

One of the lessons that I've learned from my previous relationships is that *love isn't enough*. That means to me that I can love someone and that loving of him or her may not be enough to sustain the relationship. Although it may sound counter-intuitive there is more to maintaining a relationship than love, and that's been one of the most difficult lessons I've had to learn in my life.

In most of my relationships, the point at which we decide to have sex is sooner rather than later. That's partly because most of my relationships have started when I developed an emotional attachment to someone with whom I only initially intended to have sex. Before the morality police start donning their flashlights and nightsticks, I will acknowledge that there are other ways of entering relationships that many people advocate (while few actually practice consistently).

My decisions to have sex with people with whom I'm not in a long-term committed relationship do not eliminate the possibility of intimacy, love, affection, or commitment in the sexual encounters I have. In fact, what I'm describing is the way in which those things do show up, oftentimes unexpectedly, with people I meet just to fuck. In part because of my internalization of social messages, I forget how profound and intimate an immediate sexual encounter with someone can be. In forgetting that reality, I frequently underestimate the potential of those encounters then I wake up next to someone and a deep emotional, spiritual connection has been made without any other aspects of the foundation of an ongoing relationship.

Let me try an analogy here to help illustrate the situation. If you have the experience of having a God-given talent (a talent that requires some skills to perform but that comes naturally to you) that is just exceptional, you know that in performing this talent you can really experience a "larger-than-myself" sense of reality. When performing your talent, you and the talent become one entity. There's a synchronicity that develops. It's an orgasmic feeling. But without training in the skills associated with performing that talent, without disciplined practice at the talent you begin to demonstrate unpredictability and a lack of control in the quality and consistency of your performance. You have a divinely inspired talent but you don't have the skill training to sustain the talent. That's what having a deep emotional, spiritual connection with someone without any additional foundation for the relationship is.

It can be very, very painful too. You've already established a significant bond/connection and now you have to discover if you and the other person(s) know how to maintain and support the connection, are capable of maintaining and supporting the connection, and are interested in maintaining and supporting the connection. Damn! Coming to terms with the answers to those questions can work you the fuck out.

It trips me the fuck out when a night that started as great sex turns into several weeks and I have a lover with whom I'm trying to build a relationship. Some people (ex-members of the morality police or relatives of the members of the morality police) advise us to not have sex so early with people, take some time to get to know someone first before having sex, learn about our and other people's capacity to have a relationship before having sex, etc. While I think there is some merit in such advice, I also believe that the erroneous underlying assumption in that advice is that those things don't happen when sex is introduced earlier in the relationship. I also believe that if sex is going to be a part of the relationship you need to be having sex to thoroughly explore the contours of the budding relationship.

In addition to the education and support available to people to engage in safer sex practices and to delay sex on the road to developing a relationship, there needs to be more support for people when emotional and spiritual connection happens as a result of a one-night stand, anonymous sexual encounter, or immediate sexual encounter. Rather than assuming that no emotional and spiritual intimacy and connection is possible when people choose to have sex in these ways, we need to help people deal with the situation when it occurs. That will require a broader, less limited sense of morality and sexual ethics than is currently dominant in US discourses on sexuality.

MONOGAMY IS A MUST!
A POST-MODERN,
NEO-COLONIAL IMPERATIVE

While talking to my godson-daughter one day, I came to realize that *sexual monogamy* is a necessity for anyone currently living in the West. I used to question the a priori nature monogamy appeared to play in the way people around me talked about long-term, sexual relationships. Until that discussion with him, I'd never been able to understand why sexual monogamy held such a powerful position in the way people conceive of certain relationships. Other than as a strategy to minimize the experience of feelings of jealousy, insecurity, or envy, I'd never seen any value in the dominant role monogamy plays in the structuring of many relationships (yes, I know that some people use monogamy as an

HIV and AIDS prevention strategy). But that day I finally got it.

Monogamy is a way of creating fidelity in a relationship. Merriam-Webster's dictionary defines fidelity as, *"the quality or state of being faithful."* The dictionary goes on to say, *"Fidelity implies strict and continuing faithfulness to an obligation, trust, or duty."* Wow. As I look at the concept of fidelity, I am impressed by how important that is to me. I am also struck by how little fidelity I see around me:

- Corporate executives are lying, cheating, and screwing over their investors and shareholders.
- Civilians in control of the US military are exploiting that relationship in the interests of profit and political gain.
- Corporations "downsize" their workforce in the interest of profits dramatically limiting the level of job security workers have.
- Religious leaders preach one set of moral codes for their parishioners while they are practicing another set for themselves.
- The US Supreme Court, originally designed to work independent of partisanship and to uphold the rule of law, has become an agent of the most cynical political interests.
- Multinational corporations move around the globe from one exploited local workforce to another seeking conditions that are more and more favorable to profits and less and less favorable to human rights.
- News agencies collude in the fabrication of sensational stories posing as news that distract their readership/ viewership from issues that have a real, direct impact upon their lives.

Our obligations and duties to each other are terribly strained. We can read about betrayals of the social trust perpetrated by institutions and powerbrokers in this society almost daily. We are more suspicious, more cynical, and more faithless (in the face of heightened religiosity) than ever before. No wonder we continue to insist on monogamy in our personal sexual relationships. Left without any sense of fidelity in any aspect of public life, we retreat to the fidelity found in our visions of monogamy in our private lives.

Rather than symbols of this society's civilization, greatness, and evolution, monogamy and our obsession with monogamy are symbols of the decay of Western society. Monogamy is Western society's last shred of social fidelity. Abandoned as a consequence of the dismantling of social fidelity within our social institutions, we dangle, on the edge of the precipice of the decline of the West as an imperial power, clinging to the idea of lifelong, long term sexual exclusivity as our last best hope of surviving alienation, isolation, and loneliness.

How pathetic is that?

SEX: WHAT'S NEXT?

I see sex in numerous areas of people activity. It's in advertising, entertainment, religion, and law. There are conferences, professional organizations, and academic disciplines devoted to the subject of sex. There are sex magazines, sex journals, sex comic books, sex novels, and sex e-zines. With Foucault's assessment of the proliferation of Western "discourses of sex" in mind, I can't help but wonder at this moment: With all this *talk* about sex, is our sex any better?

Certainly, I don't think my sex is. I can't remember the last time I had sex with someone and was surprised by something s/he did sexually. I know there are those among you who would challenge the implicit association that unpredictability means better sex. In fact, some would argue that familiarity and consistency contribute to the quality of sex. Does someone really want to go into sex fearing it could be hit or miss (no pun intended)? Having a stable partner that you know can deliver over and over again in the same way—in a way that is really pleasurable to you—is obviously appealing. But I'm not talking about situations of ongoing relationship. Those contexts frequently develop larger spheres of relatedness and togetherness and can also drive or undermine sexual spontaneity.

I'm talking here about the sexual scripts we carry with us into the sexual moment. Do you suck dick, eat pussy, lick ass? Do you swallow? Are you into spitting? Do you want things clean or dirty? Smelling sweet or raunchy? Do you usually make the first move or are you the closer? Some would say that all those things depend upon the person. But I wonder how many of those things really depend on the *kind of person* rather than the person. Do we play to certain kinds of characters differently because of their gender, age, size, level of social desirability, apparent interest in us, economic class, educational level, etc?

I'm asking these questions, not for mere academic exercise, but because I am plagued and belabored by them. Very often, because of the (non)sexual, social persona I project and because of my physical stature, I'm typecast into the role of a particular character by potential and probable sexual partners. Like so many bad pop fiction storylines, a script, unspoken and unwritten, is constructed that places the two of us, three of us, four of us, or how many are present at the time, within a set of given boundaries that limit possible pleasures.

The gay boys among you are probably saying to yourselves right now, "Oh, he's just a *top* that wants to get fucked." (BTW, ever notice no gay boys ever say, "Oh he's just a *bottom* that really wants to top.") And the straight peoples are probably saying, "He's confused. He probably wants some chick to put on a strap-on and fuck him." Actually, what I'm trying to surface right now comes from a different place of frustration and alienation. Though I have some idea of what I'm talking about, it's still nebulous at the same time. So take this moment with me to be unsure, tentative, and patient with the ambiguity.

Versatile and bisexual, two referential categories representing ambiguity and unrestrictedness in our everyday discussion of sexual potentiality, are themselves subject to sexual scripting. Who you should be, what you should be able to do, and why you do it are bounded by the character roles we apply to the categories. These character roles both delimit and define the sexual potentiality we expect, thereby limiting the sexual possibilities that exist.

But I want to get away from the treatment of sexual scripting through looking at labels like bisexual, versatile, gay, top, trans, man, woman, straight, bottom, etc. because I'm more intrigued by how the sexual scripting is embodied in and inscribed upon our physicality (the bodies we present to the world), our physical appearance (what the world projects onto our bodies) and in our performance of sex. I'm struggling to get around this sexual scripting and I'm trying to track its course while I'm involved in hooking up with someone. Where does the process of sexual scripting begin? Does it start at the moment I find someone attractive? Does it start the moment I know someone finds me attractive? Does it occur the moment of the first touch? Kiss? Lick? Suck? When do we make up our minds about the sexual potentiality in a sexual relationship? What does an embodied communication of that decision look like?

I acknowledge that I'm not only an object of sexual scripting but I also perform it. I've had sex with people to re-make a sexual experience I had in the past. I've also had sex with people to choreograph a fantasy sexual experience out of the reality of the sexual moment. Those were sexual scripts. When I decide what I will do sexually or won't do sexually with someone because of whom I've positioned her/him to be—based upon how s/he appears to me or because of who I've positioned myself to be—I'm sexually scripting. I know this. But I'm also asking myself how I (de)limit the sexual potentiality in my sexual relationships by the sexual scripting that I perform and the way in which I embody those decisions inside of the sexual moment.

As a trained sexologist inundated—because of my deliberately comprehensive participation in sex cultures—with sexual discourses of all sorts, I'm challenged to find the surprise and wonder I desire in the few sexual moments of which I avail myself. In part because of the social proliferation of all things sexual with very little substance in the United States and also in part because of my own struggles with sexual scripting, I find myself bored and stagnated. I'm looking to be surprised, to have my assumptions challenged, to find the disconcerting, yet immensely gratifying, plot twist in a sexual story I'm sharing with someone whether it lasts for a couple of hours, one night, or for years.

WHAT RIGHT-WING, FUNDAMENTALIST CONSERVATIVES COULD ARGUE IF THEY WERE SMART

I had what I think was a six-hour phone conversation with a former boyfriend triggering the coalescing of some ideas that have been percolating in/around me for a little bit now.

As a self-identified sex-affirming, sex radical committed to a thoughtful, conscientious practice of my sexual desires no matter how kinky and socially transgressive, I've given myself permission to define my sexual values and ethics independent of the sanitizing influence of mainstream dogma from JudeoChristianIslamic science, religion, and law. I've relied upon my careful study of non-Western and Western cultural frameworks throughout various periods of human history and the direction of my personal resources (will, desire, intuition, ancestral wisdom, etc.) in developing a deeply personal set of sexual values and ethics.

Exploring practices like polyamory, BDSM, monogamy, group sex, ménage tois, etc., I've had opportunities to construct my desire and the practice of my desire in sexual contexts that have challenged a priori expectations about the nature of sexual-intimate relationships/interactions. In other words, I've had sex in all kinds of contexts and therefore I feel more authoritative in advancing an argument for sexual social responsibility than the moralizing police who have influenced or governed sexual social policy in this country for too fucking long.

So what does a sex-affirming, sexual social responsibility look like? Rather than pathologize, criminalize, or marginalize any sexual practice between consenting persons, I want to call our attention to the spiritual implications of our sexual practices. The religious right would have us consider the degree to which any sex practice conforms to the norms and values set up by the dogma of their religious system. Social conservatives would do the same using the socio-cultural norms and values that dominate the landscape of this society.

I want to look—not at the dogma or social standards and beyond issues of sexually transmitted infection and disease questions—to the relational nature of our sex practices on a spiritual level. I believe that sex can create a moment of spiritual and psychic engagement. This engagement can last beyond the moment of sexual activity. So, for example, when someone swallows my cum, s/he is not just ingesting my sperm and semen. S/he is ingesting: my *karma* or *shai*, a distillation of my spirit, my *chi*, and my *ankh*. The same is true for when someone receives my cum in her pussy or his/her ass. Each time I am bathed in the menstrual blood of a lover I am forever changed, becoming myself plus the addition of another's essence carried through blood.

Our saliva, vaginal fluids, semen, blood, and sweat, exchanged during our sex, carry more than the mechanisms of disease as branded by the Western public health industrial complex, and more than the sociopolitical meaning suggested by Western postmodernist discourse, and even more than the genetic material mapped and colonized by Western genome imperialists. They carry, or rather, they are pieces of us—pieces of ourselves that we leave in people's mouths, on people's stomachs. They are bits and pieces of ourselves, our spiritual essences, left with and in everyone that we've fucked. These bits and pieces are mixing with them, their spiritual essences, and forming new combinations, possibilities, and challenges to consider in our interpersonal relations and connectivity.

What then are the responsibilities that my sexual partner(s) and I share to ourselves and each other given these combinations, possibilities, and challenges? I ask this question with a hope that our answers don't lead to a (re)inscribing of dogma in a new form that replaces or (re)positions the current dogma that exists. I seek instead a clarification of what we are to each other as co-participants in sex and a journey into the psychic and spiritual ramifications of the sexual moment.

Our responsibilities to ourselves are to listen to what our bodies, our emotions, our thoughts, and our spirits are telling us while we are having sex. That requires a critical, embodied consciousness. We are responsible for entering into a sexual experience with integrity and authenticity. We are responsible for asking serious questions of our partners and ourselves and answering seriously the questions of our partners. We are responsible for taking heed to the lessons we learn from our sexual experiences and incorporating the wisdom from those lessons into our subsequent sexual choices.

YOU KNOW YOU'RE A FREAK WHEN

I am a **Freak**. I'm proud to be. But I believe there's a misconception amongst the general public about what a **Freak** is and what it means to be a **Freak**. Looking at personal ads and listening to general flirtatious conversation, I've gathered that most people don't have a clue of what it means to be a **Freak**. So in the interest of shared understanding of and appreciation for the role of the **Freak** in society, I am going to share a few notes on the topic. Learn and enjoy.

You know you are a **Freak** when people that you know and people that you don't know call you and ask, "What you got going on tonight?" knowing in their loins that you have planned a salacious evening that they must attend.

You know you are a **Freak** when your bed has a plastic mattress cover on it at all times because you never know when you might use your bed as an oil-wrestling mat or piss play area.

You know you are a **Freak** when books by author Samuel R. Delany (*The Mad Man, Hogg: A Novel, Times Square Red, Times Square Blue*) describe, chronicle, or foreshadow your life.

You know you are a **Freak** when you start to yawn when you read, listen to, or observe what most people define as **Freak**.

You know you are a **Freak** when your mother comes over to your house to get condoms.

You know you are a **Freak** when your relationship ends with a lover and s/he has to attend a debriefing session like an astronaut, secret agent, or soldier returning from a mission.

You know you are a **Freak** when your lovers leave the relationship craving the very things and types of people that they said disgusted them when you first met them.

You know you are a **Freak** when people who were only momentary lovers (one night stands) send you gifts every now and again to just thank you for the experience.

You know you are a **Freak** when nothing comes to mind when you're asked, "What sexual fantasies do you have that you haven't yet experienced?"

You know you are a **Freak** when simple dinner conversation includes words like "injaculation," "clitoris," "butt plugs," and "foot fetish."

You know you are a **Freak** when your friends have to clarify the intended purpose of the kitchen items/utensils in your home before using them: "What do you use this turkey baster/tong/whisk/spatula for?"

You know you are a **Freak** when the paddles hanging from your ceiling don't have the insignia of any fraternity or sorority but definitely look well worn.

You know you are a **Freak** when you notice (and everyone else doesn't notice) that everyone at the meeting is attempting to hide the knowing smile emerging across their lips from having had the pleasure of your "company."

You know you are a **Freak** in your bones. It's a calling. You don't need anyone to tell you that you are a **Freak**. You may need someone to call your attention to what's already there inside you.

DE-FIEND-ING POLYAMORY: UNPACKING THE CINDERELLA/SNOW WHITE MYTH AND HETEROSEXUAL IDEAL

For many of us, the concept of a relationship between adults who love each other can be for the most part characterized as "the couple." It involves two adults and no more than two adults. There is an expectation of sexual monogamy if not emotional monogamy. To explore further this idea, these two people eventually meet after searching for their "soul mate" or at least remaining vigilant for their "soul mate" until one day they meet "the one" and know they are "in love."

I often call this idea "The Heterosexual Ideal" or "The Cinderella/ Snow White Myth." The fairytales of Cinderella, Snow White, and their fairytale cousins that many of us learned as children are great teachers of this idea. Whether str8 or not, we were educated into perceiving the possibilities of relationships through this myth. When we are old enough to make decisions about creating and developing relationships with others, we frequently take this as an opportunity to act upon our learning of the myth whether we identify as str8 or not.

Unfortunately, there is very little discussion of these fairytales as communications of social information about relationships. What does it mean for Snow White's ass to remain in a coma, asleep, inactive, and unaware until the right man comes around to kiss her ass awake? Why are all the men—other than Prince Charming—in Snow White's life (the seven dwarfs) emotionally incomplete, stagnant, or rigid? Why is the Prince in Cinderella forced to walk around the community trying to find the right woman to physically fit into his mold of feminine perfection?

These fairytales teach us ways of being in relationship and creating/developing relationships that we have not fully explored individually or collectively. Even more dangerous is the fact that these fairytales leave us with big expectations once we are in a relationship with "the one"—to live happily ever after. There is no mention of the loss of sexual lust, the negotiation of how to live with each other, or what happens when couple's counseling becomes a necessity. All you need to do is find the right one and everything else will work itself out if you follow the lessons implied in these stories.

Where are the other options from which we can choose in an informed, conscious way? Where are the models of how to create and develop a consensual and committed polygamous relationship (three or more persons)? A consensual, committed communal relationship (group)? Where are the examples of a woman in a committed long-term relationship with several men? Where are the exemplars of a man in a long-term committed, consensual relationship with a man and a woman?

I am not saying "The Heterosexual Ideal" is invalid. My question is more about whether our attempts to aspire to that ideal are based upon our unconsciousness with regard to the various ways of being in relationship with each other or a conscious, informed choice rooted in our holistic assessment of the consequences of the options available to us. I have made a conscious and informed decision that Snow White isn't for me. Give me the Black Funk, 'cause for me that's where my home is, my love is, and my sex is.

I practiced polyamory in the context of a committed relationship that I co-maintained for 10 years. I am also attracted to and have had sex with women and men. I tell you this to be transparent about where I'm coming from in my discussion of these issues both in terms of experience and perspective.

Over the years, I have heard many times that polyamory, i.e., the practice of engaging in committed relationships that include more than two people, is not feasible or is not appropriate for us as emotionally mature, evolved human beings. I think it's important that before people make statements about the lack of feasibility in creating and successfully maintaining polyamorous relationships they should ask themselves what personal characteristics, traits, abilities, capacities, behaviors, approaches, and decisions it would take to create and successfully maintain polyamorous relationships that are healthy and empowering.

Once they do that and look at their list, they might be surprised at how useful these things would be in monogamous relationships. It may be difficult for some to even generate a list because they are not able to step outside the relationship paradigm that they have been taught, Christian heterosexual monogamy. For many, anything that doesn't fit that paradigm is automatically problematic because they don't know anything else. Even those who tinker with the idea often fail to realize that critical to the success of polyamorous relationships is being rigorously aware of how you have internalized so deeply heterosexual monogamy ideals—internalized to the degree that everything you see, you see through that lens—and how useless much of that previous learning will be in working outside the paradigm. It's like thinking that you can use the same grammatical rules of English to speak Zulu as long as you use Zulu vocabulary. The shit doesn't work. You have to use Zulu grammatical rules with Zulu vocabulary to speak Zulu and to really speak it well you need to have a Zulu sensibility as the foundation for the grammatical rules and vocabulary.

A lot of the criticism that people make of polyamory comes out of their own pain, hurt, and unfilled and unmet needs in monogamous, oftentimes serial monogamous, relationships. They use their experiences from serial monogamous relationships to denounce or call into question polyamorous relationships. That is a flawed argument. Many don't see the possibility that had they have been practicing polyamory they may have had a more positive experience.

Polyamorous relationships are hard work; any good relationship is. My former partner and I had to directly confront our jealousies, insecurities, inadequacies, selfishness, self-centeredness, feelings of incompleteness and loneliness, etc. Polyamory helped me to cultivate more feelings of interdependence, compassion, acceptance, self-awareness, self-love, trust, commitment, passion, mutual respect, and devotion. It was not easy. Is there anything in life that is worth having that is easy to achieve?

From my perspective, the real challenge to the sustainability and health of polyamorous relationships in this society is the lack of social support. There are a number of ways that make this society inhospitable for polyamorous relationships including laws, customs, and social practices. Polyamorous marriage is outlawed across the country. Health care policies, insurance terms, and property rights are all written in ways that are antagonistic to polyamorous relationships. In addition to the *de jure* hostility, there is the *de facto* hostility that is expressed by the average person's approach and understanding of polyamory.

People who want to initiate and/or maintain polyamorous relationships must work considerably harder to make those relationships work in the face of the social hostility and antagonism that they face. Logistically, there is a lot with which to deal in establishing such a relationship. For the most part, if the person is new to polyamory, s/he must undergo a significant re-education process to learn the worldview, language, values, ethics, and principles of polyamory. Assuming you find someone who already has undergone such a re-education, you still have to explore the degree to which you are all on the same page about what polyamory means to each of you and what you are seeking in the relationship.

Polyamory doesn't mean being uncommitted. Actually, polyamorous relationships can be the most explicated form of committed relationship in that frequently they are consciously and deliberately created with large amounts of discussion as a means of coming to agreement about the nature, parameters, and expectations of the relationship as well as the people in the relationship. Of course this is not the case in all polyamorous relationships. The kinds of polyamorous relationships I have been speaking about throughout this essay are ones that are entered into by mutual consent and for mutual fulfillment. There are those polyamorous relationships that have been forged through patriarchal cultural tradition and that may benefit one member disproportionately more than the other members of the relationship. Those are not the kinds of polyamorous relationships for which I am primarily speaking.

Polyamorous relationships can be non-capitalist, non-patriarchal, and sex-positive ways of configuring intimate, sexual human relations. It means stepping outside of the love-as-ownership paradigm and embracing a paradigm of love-as-authentic-engagement. In this paradigm, intimacy does not require possession and commitment does not require exclusivity. Intimacies are acts of engagement and commitments are acts of integrity. None of these acts occur, however, in a vacuum. For polyamorous relationships to work on a large scale, we need to create more spaces of support, even if it means creating our own communities where we can practice the love that we desire.

GET RID OF THEM: 10 TIPS FOR IDENTIFYING A RELATIONSHIP THAT IS A WASTE OF YOUR TIME

Tip 1 - If s/he continues to talk about her/his friends negatively and tells you that "they aint shit," get rid of her/him. Their behavior indicates that either they don't respect themselves enough to get rid of problematic people in their life or they have no capacity to establish a meaningful, loving relationship with someone at this point in their life. Get rid of them.

Tip 2 - If s/he, in describing past relationships, can only identify what the other person did wrong, get rid of her/him. Their behavior indicates an inability to take responsibility for events in their life. This will probably manifest in your interaction with them: blaming you for shit, doing fucked-up things and never being able to apologize, etc. Get rid of them.

Tip 3 - If s/he has fucked up relationships with every member of her/his family, get rid of her/him. Unless they are in therapy and spiritual intervention for this, there is a high probability that the pain, alienation, and rage caused by the situation will manifest in their non-familial, intimate relationships and you'll be the target of such negativity. Get rid of them.

Tip 4 - If s/he requires you to constantly compliment her/him or reassure her/him of their attractiveness, intelligence, sexual performance, creativity, etc., get rid of her/him. They obviously have not yet reached a point in which they are comfortable in their own skin or grounded in a sense of self. They will drain you for all your worth until there's no more of you left to give and then they'll be on to the next person to supplement their sense of self-worth. Get rid of them.

Tip 5 - If s/he offers no opinion about where to go or what to do, waiting instead for you to make all the decisions, get rid of her/him. Unless the person is a BDSM sub/slave, having no opinion is like having no soul, no substance, and no place in the world. Who needs to be with someone like that? Get rid of them.

Tip 6 - If s/he continually suggests ways you can change or improve yourself to make you more desirable in their eyes, get rid of her/him. They have you on a renovation/refurbishment plan and that means they're not satisfied with who you currently are. Get rid of them.

Tip 7 - If s/he talks about having a committed, long term relationship with you and the two of you originally hooked up on some screwing around, DL, sneak tip, OPP type shit, get rid of her/him. They obviously have a problem with consistency of action and thought and have failed to see that how you start something affects how something will progress or end. Get rid of them.

Tip 8 - If s/he does not know how to act toward your friends, i.e., too damn nice or too damn standoffish, get rid of her/him. They will end up fucking your friend(s) or making your time around them unpleasant. Why would you want to put up with either of these scenarios? Trust me on this one; I know this one all too well. Get rid of them.

Tip 9 - If you are with her/him because s/he represents everything (e.g., young, experienced, worked out, intelligent, wealthy, car-owning, goal-oriented, popular, masculine, feminine, etc.) that you wish you were but aren't, get rid of her/him. You need to either learn to love who and what you are or become that person that you wish you were. If you never do either, you will grow to resent them and neither you nor they deserve that. Get rid of them before they wise up and get rid of you.

Tip 10 - If s/he gives you reason to use a list like this as an excuse to do what you know you need to do, get rid of her/him. Yes, they may have their good points. Yes, they really do look good in those.... Yes, they really turn you out. But, if you're seriously questioning the situation, then you've already acknowledged that something is not right. Get rid of them.

These tips are no substitution for therapy and/or spiritual intervention. If you are really going through it in a relationship, please seek out the appropriate assistance and support.

SEXUAL COURAGE: THE ENDURING LEGACY OF EMMETT TILL AND THE WAR OF TERROR

My definition of sexual courage is acting from a place of sexual power, self-awareness, and self-love in a context in which it is not so easy to do. Every time I am sexual with another man I am exercising sexual courage because I have internalized the messages that I received growing up that said sex with another man would lead to death (male-male sex=HIV=AIDS=DEATH). So when I act to love another man physically, I am challenging a social structure that still exists and that became, as I grew up, a part of my internal scripting.

The hype that has been generated around HIV/AIDS has caused

many of us—those who have tested HIV positive and those who have tested HIV negative—to approach HIV/AIDS with terror and horror. HIV and AIDS have affected our sexual lives in countless ways. I know it has mine. I grew up in an age in which HIV/AIDS was a part of my sexual vocabulary before I had a chance to even get into some ass or pussy. I have confronted the choice to have sex with someone who I knew had tested positive.

I understand the terror and horror that many feel about the possibility of being exposed to HIV. Anal sex with someone who is HIV positive significantly increases the chances of exposure. Not using a condom increases those chances even more. Many of us just want to be safe and I can appreciate that. But sex isn't safe. Life isn't safe. Period. No matter how many tests your partners take, no matter how honest your partners are with you, safety or comfort for that matter are not rights that you or I have. But we do have sexual courage to draw upon—acting from a place of sexual power, self-awareness, and self-love.

I exercised sexual courage when I decided to own my love of other men while in a deeply fulfilling relationship with a woman and did so openly with her knowledge. I feel I exercised sexual courage by finally acknowledging my desire to sexually venture outside our relationship. If I was going to own my sexuality, I couldn't possess her sexuality. I, therefore, had to offer my jealousy and insecurities about her venturing outside of the relationship as down payments on my sexual liberation.

I've exercised sexual courage when I've decided to be honest about my sexual desires for someone despite feeling unworthy of his or her potential sexual attraction to me. I've exercised sexual courage when I've done something sexual that felt natural and good to me even though it was not the norm or what's expected in the straight community or the gay community or the Black community or the (fill in the blank) community.

Acting with sexual courage hasn't been all fun and games. It has meant serious work on my part. It has meant dealing with the social and personal consequences of the principled actions that I've taken. My actions are not taken in the absence of fears of the consequences but in the face of my fear because I wanna be free. I wanna be who I am wholly. I wanna love me and I truly want to be in relationship with others in peace, passion, and pleasure.

Years ago, when the brother got beat in the head at Morehouse College by his brother Morehouse student for allegedly looking at the latter in the bathroom, it raised a number of critical issues for me. We do shit to ourselves around our own sexuality. Morehouse brothers have been fucking with each other for years. It's been an all-male learning community for how long? So already every man there has made a decision to co-exist in an all-male homosocial environment for 4 or more years. Out of all of those men—admittedly a self-select group— there logically has to be a disproportionate number of men who are homosexually-inclined in addition to being interested in a homosocial learning community than would exist in mixed-gender educational populations.

Although the brother has publicly denied it, consider for a moment the possibility that the brother was looking at his brother-student because he was attracted to him, i.e., the look was sexual in nature. Also, consider for a moment the possibility that the brother who committed the assault with the bat was also himself attracted to other men but, as the son of a minister, he could not and did not want to be *outed* or *cruised* at that moment, in that place. If these things were true but none of us knew them to be true because both brothers were attempting to stay undercover because that's the sexual culture that exists at the if-you-know-the-deal-you-know-niggas-is-fucking-at-Morehouse College, what kinds of discussions would we need to have to create the safety for people to be a part of the discussion and benefit from the discussion while being at very different places in their own sexual development and consciousness?

I ask this question because it relates to the issue of sexual courage. Because we in communities of color continue to make our own Emmett Tills, I believe we demonstrate sexual courage when we make decisions and take actions to sexually transgress the dominant sexual order in those communities. When I act from the place of sexual power, self-awareness, and self-love—even when it goes against the proscribed norms in my community, I believe I am helping to create space for others to do the same, shattering the rules and boundaries that keep us in bondage. When I attempt to impose my sexual values on others, I become an agent of sexual oppression. When I collaborate with the heterosexualizing of an environment that is composed of people of various sexualities, I become a collaborator to sexual oppression. So rather than just remembering Emmett Till, I choose to ask myself two questions: how are you transgressing the sexual order and how many Emmett Tills have you made today?

For years, men who have sex with men taught or studied at and graduated from Morehouse without challenging the heterosexualizing of the institutional narrative. Too many Morehouse men of various sexualities kept the sexual diversity of Morehouse a secret as though there should be shame rather than pride in it. They helped to maintain the sexual Jim Crow of Morehouse. Those who chose to exercise sexual courage at Morehouse contributed to the tearing down of the walls that bounded the sexual lives of Morehouse men.

We are living during a period of war, a war of terror, of which we have to be aware. We are being taught how to be accustomed to fear and being afraid. We are told to be afraid of HIV, STIs, homosexual sex, DL men, being *outed*, growing old and alone, gaining weight around our stomachs and midsections, losing erections, ejaculating prematurely, etc. There is little in the way of education on sexual courage, i.e., acting from the place of sexual power, self-awareness, and self-love. Instead, we are encouraged to attack what scares us—lynch it, bomb it, or hit it in the head with a bat. How's that working for us?

Far be it for me to appear as though I'm discouraging political violence but here's why violence as a method isn't the right way to go in sexual liberatory struggle. The purpose of homophobia and heterosexism, like sexism and the oppression of African people and people of color, is to attack and exploit the body. Women, Black/Brown folks, and same-sex lovers are attacked and oppressed because of who we are, how our bodies move in the world, and how our love and fucking celebrates and glorifies the body and life. Such celebration and glorification of life is not cool because the agenda of the social order is the management of resources (capital resources such as currency and land, natural resources such as precious metals and fossil fuels, and human resources such as babies who will be future employees and soldiers). Our way of being in the world challenges that social agenda. Our revolutionary activity is our sex, our dance, our movement because they glorify the body and life.

Violence—as in attacks on the body and on life—would only be doing what the social system is already doing—attacking the body and life. If you want to retaliate against oppression, cultivate your capacity to fuck as a liberated, authentic, and integrated person. Learn to glorify and celebrate the body and life deeply and richly in your sex and we will fuck this system into obsolescence. (Yes, it is 2:30 in the morning when I'm writing this. No, I haven't been smoking weed. No, I haven't been reading Robert Anton Wilson lately. Yes, I am a crazy motherfucker.)

Audre Lorde advised us that if we are to create a truly liberatory reality, we cannot uncritically adopt the methods that created the systems of oppression in the first place. Instead, by consciously drawing upon our indigenous resources, we can craft both a means and a vision of liberation that is liberating. Our sensuality, our erotics, can and should play their parts. I am not speaking here of a nihilistic, selfish, and egocentric wallowing in our carnal desires. I am speaking here of the difficult and necessary work of decolonizing our bodies and desires. This work requires a daily practice of authenticity and integrity. It requires critical self-reflection and sexual courage to act based upon what we learn from our reflections.

BDSM

Sadomasochism and bondage and domination/submission have always been things that I felt uncomfortable exploring too deeply in my sex life because I thought they were some white folks shit and more importantly I felt that if I did I would be enacting the legacy of the slave experience in the United States.

Although I had these feelings, I also had feelings of interest, lust, and desire around BDSM. It was a part of my sexual experiences. My girlfriend once handcuffed me and threw me into a walk-in closet where she punched me, squeezed my nipples and dick, tortured me and mashed her pussy into my face forcing me to lick and suck on her clit and labia. I was so aroused by the torture I eventually broke free of the handcuffs writhing in total ecstasy.

Another time a causal conversation with a brother led us into a hot ass sadomasochism/domination scene. I blindfolded him and laid him on a hardwood floor in a candlelit room. I punched him in the stomach, slapped his face with my dick, and pulled at his nipple piercings and Prince Albert. Later, I opened his ass up and fucked him with my foot, getting 3-4 toes in him and making him squirm. I eventually picked up one of the candles in the room and brought it close to his face. The illumination from the candles coupled with the sensation of heat against his skin made him wince. I stood above him and began to let hot wax drip on him as I played with his dick and ass. When his chest, abs, and dick had been adequately covered in wax, I fucked him against the backdrop of his moans and screams.

My sex has included piss play, simulated rape, and other forms of sex that are often associated with BDSM. I'm not into the wearing of leather or the intricate system of rules/norms/codes of the leather scene. I think that too often the people I've seen in those settings get so caught up in the props that they forget about or are ignorant of the ability for someone to just inhabit the role of a Dom or a sub without needing any device or prop; a person's skin can exude the energy of the role so much so that it can call your body to experience it in the way it desires. That is what I try to do, what I aspire to do.

At the same time I am aware of the sociohistorical implications of BDSM. I recognize that we live in a society in which the BDSM fantasies of some (males, white folks) get to be enacted in non-sexual, real life through the political, economic, and social systems which exist because of the social power they enjoy due to sexism, white supremacy, and capitalism. I also recognize that I have been socialized to desire and seek out that which is sadomasochistic, dominating within patriarchal, European society and that my sex is informed by that socializing. As a male, I am privileged to play out being dominant or being dominated, being sadistic or masochistic as a result of my being gendered male in a way that someone who is not gendered male cannot. My racial identity as a Black man contradicts those privileges because of the way race and gender intertwine to make Black men both slaves and slavemasters, givers of pain and receivers of pain, in this society.

Rather than blindly follow the directions of my desires or repress them, I choose to consciously and critically explore my desires, to learn their lessons, and to share them to enrich my experiences with other people.

LOVE, AFFECTION, FUCKING, AND ROMANCE

I have, often, heard brothers who have sex with other brothers propose, argue, or infer that long-term monogamous relationships (LTR) between two men are more likely to contain shared intimacy and affection than is the case with one-night stands, sex party interactions, or other less on-going interactions. The goal for many of us, they would argue, would be to create a LTR with that one brother we can call ours—grow old together, share resources together, and develop together.

I applaud brothers who find what they need in those kinds of relationships and who have the skills to create and develop them. At the same time, I don't believe that those relationships are the only ones where I can find shared intimacy and affection. Whether in one night, a couple hours, or a lifetime, whether it be as lovers, fuck buddies, or bois, men of African ancestry can share intimacy and affection to the degree and in the contexts they choose. We need only to make a commitment to be involved with each other at that level to make it happen.

Personally, when I'm fucking another man I'm there to experience him as a whole being—body, mind, and soul. To tell me that there is no real sense of affection, commitment, intimacy, etc. is to deny my experience of sex in the way I experience it. To offer up long-term monogamous relationships as the only true source of intimacy, caring, love, affection, and commitment is to deny the many long-term monogamous relationships that have been robbed of the possibility of emotional intimacy or affection because the people involved don't have the skills to be emotionally intimate or affectionate or have prioritized other aspects of a relationship over intimacy and affection. Many of us, regardless of sexual practice or orientation, lack the skills to be intimate or affectionate. LTRs offer us ongoing opportunities to develop and practice those skills but they don't guarantee the existence of intimacy and commitment nor are LTRs the only contexts to develop the skills of intimacy, commitment, affection, etc.

I am also frustrated by the inference that long-term monogamous relationships are the only form of relationship. Sex is a relationship. I think—because we spend so little time, in this society, actually developing our sexual skills—the relational aspect of sex gets severely overlooked and under-examined. Two or more persons coming together to engage in sexual activity is no less and no more profound or important than two or more people coming together to engage in a long-term, monogamous relationship. The consequences for the individuals involved in either of those two acts—and for society—are no less significant.

I am concerned that we not be herded into making the erroneous choice between being freaky/being sexually exploratory OR being in relationship. Life is a lot less black and white (either/or) and a lot more Black Funk (both/and). Two people who have just met in a darkened room to have sex can have a relationship, an engagement, or an exchange at that moment that is limited to sex. Sex is just one of many levels on which we can/do connect. We have, too often, bought into Victorian notions of sex that limit our understanding of the multiple roles and levels upon which sex can play.

As an Afrocentrist, I don't put as much stock as others might in everything that comes out of a Western cultural framework. I believe that if it did so much for them, the planet wouldn't be in the condition that it is. As Queen Mother Audre Lorde said, "The master's tools will never dismantle the master's house." There are individuals in the world for whom the Western concept called "romance" has absolutely no meaning or value. And yet, for them, life is good. Imagine that, life without the concept of romance. There are people who get married in cultures of arranged marriages. These are people who don't have as much access to the materialism of the West and place more value on things like cooperative work than a nice candlelit dinner with (plug in the name of the favorite R&B singer of the moment) playing in the background.

The concept of romance in the West oftentimes bestows a kind of specialness to people, things, and moments in time. As an African, I believe that I am a unique expression of God but I'm not special or exceptional in that egocentric way. I am made of the same material as is the rest of creation. I don't desire to have someone come into my life and bestow a specialness on me. I want them to treat me with respect and compassion. I want them to demonstrate a commitment to my well-being. And I want to reciprocate those things. I want those things to exist whether in a 10-year relationship with one person (which I have experienced) or with that fly ass brother whom I briefly meet in a darkened room.

Spirituality

THE BEATITUDES REVISITED

Blessed are the people who help each other live without judgment, assumption, criticism, or ridicule, for their souls will be filled with beauty.

Blessed are those who fight against the closing of doors, for they shall see tomorrow.

Blessed are the caregivers, for they shall blot out loneliness, isolation, and fear.

Blessed are the ferocious whose teeth rip into the ripened flesh of life, for they will always be satisfied.

Blessed are the seekers of truth, for they shall survive the pits of bullshit that trap so many along the way.

Blessed are those who work in quiet obscurity without seeking recognition or praise, for they will know the joy of accomplishment.

Blessed are those who make a daily commitment to stop abuses of themselves and others, for they will gain wisdom and happiness.

Blessed are the faithful and the hopeful who can still love after the punches, kicks, knocks, jabs, strikes, and slaps, for they will know meaningful love.

Blessed are the courageous who say no to the cattle call, for they will survive the slaughter.

WHEN YOUR DEITIES HAVE
DICKS AND PUSSIES

My spiritual life took a major leap forward when, at the age of fourteen, I was initiated into a traditional African priesthood. I had been attending a program called the Junior Engineering Club (JEC). JEC was a Saturday and summer program for young Black and Latino kids. We received help with our homework and were taught calculus, chemistry, physics, digital circuits and logic as well as Tai Chi Chuan, Hatha Yoga, meditation, and Super-reading. I enjoyed myself and excelled in my studies there. JEC was created and organized by members of the priesthood. It was one of their outreach missions. That's right, Africans can be organizers of outreach missions, not just targets of them.

179

As I learned more I became more interested in the priesthood. Eventually I was called to commit my life to the priesthood. After passing several tests and taking part in several spiritual readings, I was initiated into the *Kera Amen Ra, Het Neter Seshini Hetch Ha Nub* (Shrine of *Amen Ra*, Temple of the White and Gold Lotus). The priesthood was founded on the example of the priesthoods of ancient *Khemet* (Egypt).

The priesthood provided me with a framework for understanding myself better. From as early as I could remember I felt the signs of a mystical life. I had extremely rich relationships with the elders in my family. Those relationships continued after their transitions to ancestorship. They walked with me. I talked with them. I also had a keen ability to sense how others felt. My empathic ability hadn't been cultivated or contextualized before I entered the priesthood. I always felt that I had the potential to help people in their healing. But before the priesthood there wasn't a suitable context for me to put all these feelings that I held.

The many years of training and learning within the priesthood opened my eyes to what I had been experiencing the years prior. I was able to develop my skills and abilities. I finally had an Afrocentric framework for understanding my Self and my world. One of the aspects of African spirituality for which I am most grateful is the depiction/representation of deities. I grew up in the priesthood seeing images of divinity that were both female and male. God was female. God was male. God was female and male. The gendered nature of God in the African spiritual context was contrary to the patriarchal God I had known in Christianity and Islam. *Auset, Hetheru,* and *Mut* were just as instrumental in my life as were *Ausar, Heru,* and *Amen.*

The many images of God depicted beautiful Black women and men. These beautiful Black women and men had bodies that were sensual. Sensuality is a very important aspect of African spirituality. These Gods have dicks and pussies. *Ausar's* mummy stands with *Ausar's* Black dick bold and erect. *Auset's* Tat is worn as a belt buckle depicting the thick lips of her pussy and the firm elegance of her clit. For African spiritualists the body is of God, an aspect of divinity, and therefore worthy of the same kind of love and care we devote to the soul.

During ritual we dance and sing and celebrate with our Gods. They "mount" us and we act as conduits for their words and expression. Being mounted can be an ecstatic, orgasmic experience. The sensual power of our bodies is affirmed in our communion with our Gods. The sweat pours down the celebrant's back – twisting and turning. God adds a bump and grind – the body shakes and shivers. It's one of the most addictive experiences I've ever had. Each time I return to ritual I shudder in anticipation.

The priesthood did not become my permanent home. I eventually left. My principle reason for leaving was that I had grown beyond the point that my spiritual teachers in the priesthood could be of support. My next lesson was to understand how my specific sexual identity could be integrated into my life and into my practice as a priest. All of my spiritual teachers in the priesthood maintained heterosexual identities and their experiences outside of that context did not offer them the competence that I needed. The following eight years after leaving the priesthood I devoted to exploring this lesson.

I had my past experiences as a sexual being to assist me in this endeavor. I had been sexual with males and females since I was a kid. The naturalness of those experiences I now liken, although I didn't always, to my communion with the ancestral and spirit worlds. During those eight years, I did a lot of reflection and some reading about gender, sexuality, sex, and spirituality. I did even more conscientious, passionate fucking and sucking as an "exploration in the truths" of my body, desires, and pleasures.

My quest differed from those who have sought to find validity or legitimacy for their sexual desires, tastes, and appetites through ancient examples or historical legacy. I was seeking to integrate the Truth of my sexual desires, tastes, and appetites with the rest of my Self. Any ancient examples or historical legacies were only important to me to the degree that they provided me with models of integration. I believed the validity and legitimacy of my sexual desires, tastes, and appetites rested in their existence.

My explorations lead me to the Dagara (a tribe in West Africa) concept of *bodeme*, in English "gatekeepers" or "keepers of the gates." To my knowledge, Dr. Malidoma Somé is the first African to bring the concept of gatekeepers to the general public in the United States. The following statement is an excerpt of an interview with Somé on the subject of gatekeepers:

> The reason why I'm saying there are no such people is because the gay person is very well integrated into the community, with the functions that delete this whole sexual differentiation of him or her. The gay person is looked at primarily as a "gatekeeper." The Earth is looked at, from

my tribal perspective, as a very, very delicate machine or consciousness, with high vibrational points, which certain people must be guardians of in order for the tribe to keep its continuity with the gods and with the spirits that dwell there. Spirits of this world and spirits of the other worlds. Any person who is at this link between this world and the other world experiences a state of vibrational consciousness which is far higher, and far different, from the one that a normal person would experience. This is what makes a gay person gay. This kind of function is not one that society votes for certain people to fulfill. It is one that people are said to decide on prior to being born. You decide that you will be a gatekeeper before you are born. And it is that decision that provides you with the equipment...that you bring into this world.

(Hoff, 1993:1)

My own path has always made the notion of sexual orientation, as is categorized and identified in the West, problematic. Although who and how and why I fuck has always been important to me, it has always been important to me in a way that was different than the positions that I heard articulated out in the world. In the process of integrating my Self, I began to recognize more and more the ways in which my sexuality informed my existence and life purpose. The gatekeeper concept has most closely articulated what I've recognized about my Self. This concept of gatekeeper is so rich for me that I am still working to understand it. It was even a focus in my doctoral dissertation, *Our Bodies, Our Wisdom* (OBOW). In OBOW, I compared the concept of gatekeeper to the lives and experiences of six men of African-descent in New York City who experience same-sex desire.

Sobonfu Somé, also a member of the Dagara people, offers more wisdom about the places where gender, sexuality, and community purpose intersect among gatekeepers:

The gatekeepers stand on the threshold of the gender line. They are mediators between the two genders. They make sure that there is peace and balance between women and men. If the two genders are in conflict and the whole village is caught in it, the gatekeepers are the ones to bring peace. Gatekeepers do not take sides. They simply play the role of "the sword of truth and integrity."

There are many gates that link a village to other worlds. The only people who have access to all these gates are the gatekeepers....They have one foot in all the other worlds and the other foot here. This is why the vibration of their body is totally different from others.

(Somé, 2004)

After years of maintaining an internal priestly practice, I am now openly practicing as a priest and shaman again. Basically, that means that I'm now re-engaged in my work within the community as a priest. I needed to get to a certain place in exploring my lessons about sexuality before I could re-engage the community in a holistic way. Also, having further integrated my sexual self and gendered self with the rest of me I am able to more fully practice ritual and more fully engage the ancestral and spirit worlds. I'm able to more fully appreciate the dicks and pussies that are so much a part of African spirituality, African gods, and African people.

TRANS

I remember when transexualism and transgenderism were taboo to me. Although I could and did make myself comfortable with brothers crossdressing or taking on female physical traits like breasts, it was an intellectual process that I performed because I wanted to respect brothers needs and desires to be and do what they needed to for themselves. It is worth noting that I didn't have the same issues with female-to-male trans practice.

But my breakthrough regarding male-to-female trans practice came by observing what happened to me internally when I interacted with trans women or drag queens. I recognized that I had an internal reaction to their energy. The experience was very powerful and it required me to adjust my own personal energy to make it possible to be in the same space in a harmonious way. I attribute the discomfort I experienced to my internalization of my sexist socialization. As a man, I have learned a sense of entitlement and privilege around existing in an environment where my energy or male energy dominates. The existence of trans women and drag queens sharing the same space with me challenges that entitlement and privilege and that's part of why I was uncomfortable. I appreciate the challenge to my sexist patterns of being and doing in the world. I continue to learn from and struggle with the challenge.

Transgendered folks carry a sexual energy that was intimidating to me. As I move through the world with my own sexual energy, I unconsciously and consciously attempt to reach an energetic synergy in which we are both vibing at the same level. I'm not talking about being physically sexual here. I'm talking about energetically—how we vibe. My prejudices made it possible for transgendered folks to challenge my efforts to attain that synergetic level. I had to learn how to overcome the obstacles created by my prejudices so that I could create synergy with transgendered folks. It was about doing the work I needed to do within myself and out in the world to come to the place I am now. But I had to want to do that work. It had to be important to me and it was in part because I don't like remaining a slave to prejudices or arbitrary social constraints.

There are numerous configurations of trans-reality around the world. From the *two-spirit* in Native American culture, the *ga'tuby* in Thai culture, the *mahu* in Tahitian culture, the *waria* in Indonesian culture, to the *hijras* in Indian culture, people of color communities have expressions of gender that are broader than the female-male binary. In many of these contexts, European (Western Europe, United States, and Canada) colonization and/or cultural hegemony have fostered a climate of intracultural tension and social animosity toward people whose energies don't conform to male-female gender binaries. In the pre-colonial and traditional periods, all members of society were more likely to be valued and appreciated in many of these societies.

In fact, many indigenous peoples have creation stories in which original humankind was androgynous, i.e., both male and female. In these stories, the original or primordial humans were direct and complete representations of the Divine, an androgynous entity. As early human beings became more disconnected from their divine origins, androgyny represented a divine ideal that was out of the relative grasp of the average human being. Certain people are, however, touched by this spirit of our ancient past and blessed with the gift of androgyny or transgender.

These members of our families carry important energies for our communities. They carry a form of energy from our primordial past and offer us a glimpse into a different kind of reality. We have much to learn from the trans members of our family. But to do so we have to get past our prejudices. Trans folks are the progeny of the Mother God, the Divine Feminine. In evolutionary biology, feminine beings that give birth independent of males, i.e., by asexual reproduction, frequently produce offspring that are both female and male. Trans folks exist because of the Divine Feminine, our Mother God. She is their protector. Attack them and you are attacking Her, and you are risking the vengeance of a protective, fierce mother.

Likewise, trans folks must embrace all of their nature and not settle for what has become popularized by European/US/Canadian society, i.e., drag shows and balls. There is more to all of us than what pop culture would have us embody. As a trans person, to fully embody the energy of trans and be undeterred by pop culture and European cultural hegemony and technology (e.g., sexual reassignment surgery and hormone therapy) is to remember from where you come and from whom you come. In that context, one can be trans without ever performing a drag show, walking a ball, taking a hormone, or having a surgery. Trans is a way of being and moving in the world that troubles the waters and brings all of humanity closer to our Divine origins.

BITCH'S BREW

Stink and flow bitch
Send that musky red/brown seepage into my mouth
Send it spilling in globs of discarded flesh
making glop glop glopping sounds of gravity controlled eruptions
I want to smell the earthy stench of your meaty pit of flesh and hair
and mucous and blood and blood and blood
As I breathe in the natural aroma of your syrupy swamp,
I choke against the pressure, the heat
from the gaping wet hole between your legs

I shudder under its blanket
covering me from the inside, out
leaving me no space to relieve myself of the intensity
I drink down the promising poison to prevent my soul from
asphyxiation
salty and vile the nectar invades my mouth
and in doing so, ravages my manhood
sending shockwaves through me as I convulse over and over
burning my throat burning my stomach burning
The bitch's brew makes a cauldron of my gut
I feel her stirring her cunt concoction with the pride of a sous chef
She enables me a moment to settle into my fate
I am filled I am filled I am filled I am filled
with the spirits of this unholy ghost
served in a wicked black rose wine glass
Dry, no ice
And then she dances
with it dripping on the floor
with it dripping on the floor
with it dripping on the floor
The drops splatter leaving meaningful messages of misery
of pain of violence of decay of death
Death be not proud death be not a shroud death be another drop
of her poison nectar hitting the weather worn wood floor as she
dances
as she dances
with you with me
I can't hold onto it anymore and I feel her brew bubbling, bubbling
out my belly
seeping like sweat through virgin pores
I too add to the mess on the floor I have become a part of her
chemistry
Looking down into a pool of my own private poison
I order another round
And this time
Make it a double.

BLACK MAMA SAUCE

I am a Black profeminist/womanist. Not in the sense that most people in the West come to conceive of feminism/womanism but rooted in my experience of African spirituality, cosmology, and ontology. As such, I have frequently found myself at odds with intellectual feminists who have been schooled in feminism by way of the Western academy and also at odds with Black cultural-nationalists who have come to know what it means to be African from a secular/non-spiritual perspective. My conceptualization of Black feminism/womanism is as much tied to my experience of Black Mama Sauce as it is tied to my reading of Black Feminist Thought.

Black Mama Sauce is the term I use to give words to the energetic power of the Great Black Mother, She from whom we all have come. Many African cultural communities, including Dagara, Khemet, and Dogon, have cosmologies—creation stories or first origin mythologies—that describe a primordial beginning as a black ocean. Evolutionary theorists talk about the beginning of the universe and the beginning of life on earth in these terms, as well. In Khemet, we called her *Nu* or *Nun*. It is from this black ocean that all things emerged. The Dagara and Dogon believe that the first beings to emerge out of this black ocean were male and female, i.e., androgynous beings.

Through ritual and possession, I have experienced this black ocean and have come to know Her as the first mother, the Great Black Mother. Though we are well removed in time from the first beings emerging from Her as a black ocean, She is a presence and force that has remained significant over time.

The rise of the hegemony of masculinism, male privilege, and patriarchy has dampened our capacities to appreciate Her but their efforts to do so have also evidenced Her power. Men's will to power over the centuries has been, in part, due to their lack of complete identification with Her. Male physiology and anatomy has little that is comparable with the physiology and anatomy of the Great Black Mother. There are no obvious cycles as there are for females, no potentiality for asexual reproduction as there are for females, and generally no innate connection with the environment as there are for females. For the most part, human males, unless they are queer, have very little that connects them to the Great Black Mother.

As a consequence of this disconnection, human males, i.e., men, have constructed elaborate systems for mimicking the being and processes of the Great Mother while simultaneously developing ideologies that function as hegemonic counter-narratives antagonistic to the power and presence of the Great Black Mother in our cultures. Male rites of passage and blood sacrifices are examples of the former.

Because there are not physiological processes that occur among men that signal adulthood or maturity, male rites of passage were, in part, created to make evident the process of male adulthood and to usher in that stage of development in ways that maximize healthy human development. During rites of passage, initiated, older men take uninitiated, younger men to secluded places away from the rest of the community to imbue within them the kind of connectedness to the environment and community responsibility that is necessary for men to have in order for them to constructively participate in a community or society. These processes oftentimes involve the use of ritual, storytelling, hallucinogens, arduous, even potentially fatal trials, and other such methods that take the young men outside of regular time and everyday consciousness to a temporal place and consciousness that is most receptive to the power of the Great Black Mother.

Blood sacrifice involves the shedding of the blood of an animal (including humans) in a ritualistic context for the purpose of achieving a mystical/magical effect or goal. In various spiritual-cultural communities, chickens, hens, goats, calves, or other such beings are sacrificed so that their blood—which is considered to contain valuable psychic/spiritual energy—can be used as an ingredient in talismanic medicine and ritual. I am referring to Indigenous practices in Africa, South and Central America, and the Caribbean as well as to the Judeo-Christian traditions related to blood sacrifice.

During a ritual, I was granted the knowledge, through possession, that blood sacrifice is a product of the rise of masculinism, male privilege, and patriarchy. Prior to them, the blood that was primarily used in magic, talismanic medicine, and ritual was menstrual blood. Menstrual blood is one of the many ways women are directly connected to the Great Black Mother. On a psychic-spiritual level, menstrual blood is a part of what the primordial black ocean was. That is why it is so energetically potent and valuable.

The use of menstrual blood positioned women as central to the making of talismanic medicine and the performance of certain rituals. Men were not only dependent upon women in this regard but also dependent upon the maintenance of good and decent relationships with women in order to be given the privilege of access to a woman's menstrual blood. Blood sacrifice cut the monopoly women had as the source of blood used for magic. Though some women and men continued to use menstrual blood in the old way, many women and still larger numbers of men converted to the use of blood sacrifice. No longer do men have to depend on maintaining good and decent relationships with women to engage in certain forms of magic. No longer do women and men have to wait for the menses cycle to perform certain rituals or create certain talismans. Millions of animals and perhaps thousands of humans have been slaughtered in breaking the blood monopoly, yet Black Mama Sauce still survives.

Black Mama Sauce is menstrual blood and much more. Black Mama Sauce is Blues, Funk, and Soul music. Black Mama Sauce appears in the work of Jean Michel Basquiat. Black Mama Sauce is in the writings of Toni Morrison, Toni Cade Bambara, Alice Walker, Octavia Butler, and Ishmael Reed. Black Mama Sauce flows from the altars and shrines of juju workers, hoodoo people, and conjurers. Black Mama Sauce runs over the flesh of dancers moving in ecstatic rhythm to tribal house music. Black Mama Sauce erupts from the passionate sex of free lovers.

Black Mama Sauce is the energetic foundation for our work in Black Funk. We call forth the energy of the Great Black Mother to engage folks in the exploration of sensual awareness, sexual consciousness, erotic power, and pleasure. We do this through a reverence for Her and an appreciation for Her power. In our spaces, we make sure to build an altar/shrine to one or more of the Great Feminine Deities. I am particularly partial to the goddesses *Sekhmet* and *Heru-Het* from Khemet. *Sekhmet* is a warrior goddess, much like Hindu's *Kali*. She drinks blood and eats hearts. She is a fierce and ferocious sister born of fire. *Sekhmet* was transformed in *Heru-Het* when the former drank a portion deliberately meant to tame her. *Heru-Het* is a love goddess. Her Yoruba counterpart is *Oshun*. *Heru-Het* is also a seducer. She winds, twirls, and grinds her thick hips in hypnotic fashion. Both goddesses bless/curse us with their passion and desire. It is a challenge to drink as much of Black Mama Sauce to enjoy the fullness of the blessings of *Sekhmet* and *Heru-Het* without slipping into an overindulgence that can turn the blessing into a curse. Over years of working in this way, we, at Black Funk, have learned many lessons that have allowed us to work with these energies given their blessings and potential risks.

When I work with clients individually or in groups, I am always drawing upon Black Mama Sauce to create the context for deep engagement, critical reflection, passionate discourse, and sensitive awareness within myself and the people with whom I am working. When working with folks whose consciousnesses are more Westernized, I am rarely explicit about my use of Black Mama Sauce. I just do the work. With folks who have more of an appreciation for and awareness of Indigenous Knowledge, I am more explicit. But regardless of what others are about, I am using Black Mama Sauce, the energetic power of the Great Black Mother, to counsel, advise, facilitate, teach, or minister.

BLASPHEMING TO THE CHOIR

Sometime ago, I posted the following status message on one of my instant message buddy lists, *"Jesus was a lover of men, a man who had sex with men, and a foot fetishist. Archeologists find new evidence."* In the wake of the recent onslaught of religious dogma and ideology based heterosexism and erotophobia, I figured some of the individuals on my buddy list would chuckle. I didn't expect to receive messages like this one from DiscreetBro (I've changed the name to protect the naive), someone who I don't even know but who obviously I allowed to put me on his buddy list.

DiscreetBro: *I don't know what you've been reading but it is plainly the work of the devil. And if you don't repent and erase that garbage you have written on here, you will continue to endanger your soul to everlasting damnation!*

I responded to DiscreetBro with the following:

ME: Is that all it takes to endanger one's soul to everlasting damnation?

ME: Damn, that was easy.

ME: I thought there was a whole lot more work involved.

ME: This everlasting damnation thing must be popular among lazy ass motherfuckers.

ME: They don't have to do a whole lot and they get big results.

ME: Thanks for the info.

ME: BTW, what are you being discreet about?

DiscreetBro didn't say another word beyond his initial statement. RudeBlack (name also changed to protect the zealous) was much more willing to engage me. Here is the transcript of that conversation:

RudeBlack: u are sick

ME: ok

RudeBlack: u must get this all the time

ME: nope

RudeBlack: well u get it now and u better believe it

RudeBlack: u are sick

RudeBlack: go seek help

ME: why am I sick?

RudeBlack: i think u know why so its not necessary to speak about it

ME: why?

RudeBlack: sayin this about Jesus

ME: I didn't say it...I was repeating the report that just came out today. You didn't hear about it? It's been on yahoo.

ME: and on the news

RudeBlack: WHAT???

RudeBlack: WHAT NEWS CHANNEL?

RudeBlack: WHAT A BLASPHEMY!

RudeBlack: why you say it!

ME: Archeologists have found evidence that strongly suggests the historical Jesus of Nazareth engaged in homosexual behavior with men and had a foot fetish.
RudeBlack: where do u read it
ME: on yahoo
RudeBlack: send me the link
ME: earlier today
RudeBlack: please
RudeBlack: i cant find it
ME: i'm trying to check the other news agencies now
RudeBlack: please do
ME: you serious you hadn't heard about it today?
RudeBlack: no!
ME: i figured people would be talkin about it online
ME: ask around
ME: i'm finishing this news article on the CIA and then I'll go look again
RudeBlack: ok
RudeBlack: but tell me
RudeBlack: what do u think about it
ME: what does it matter?
RudeBlack: yes
RudeBlack: i wanna know what u think about it
ME: I'm saying my opinion...what does it matter. It doesn't add any more or less weight to my life.
ME: why? what do you think?
RudeBlack: so your opinion is that jesus was a fetishist? and homosexual?
ME: no...that's what the news article said
ME: what i'm saying in response to the news article is that it doesn't matter that he was
ME: so what
RudeBlack: but what makes you spread that news by using it as your status message?
RudeBlack: belief that the news were right?
ME: i believe that the news is news
ME: some right news is right

ME: some wrong news is wrong

ME: you don't believe the news?

RudeBlack: well you just dont admit your reason for puttin it as your status message

RudeBlack: no i dont believe most of the yahoo and cnn news

ME: i put it as my status message because it's news

ME: what news do you believe?

RudeBlack: i believe news that are actual and not news that are there to make me believe they are actual

RudeBlack: its not only matter of jesus

RudeBlack: dont u think that by using this as your message you represent some opinion and also that it can be offensive to some on your yahoo list?

ME: how do you know when news is actual and when it's not?

RudeBlack: time always tells the truth

ME: I don't think I represent an opinion. I think I represent a person, me.

RudeBlack: so u as a person is someone who think that jesus was a gay

ME: I don't ask people to put me on their buddy lists...they ask me if they can place me on their buddy list.

RudeBlack: so once they add u, for whatever reason, they have to accept your offensive messages?

ME: No, I think that a report is circulating out there in the world that says that a historical figure Jesus had sex with men and was attracted to feet.

ME: do you believe my status message is offensive?

ME: Did the status message offend you?

RudeBlack: and you personally identify with that report?

RudeBlack: yes it was very offensive i can say, very

ME: personally identify with the report? my name aint on it. I'm not collectin a check from it.

ME: why was it offensive to you?

ME: are you anti-sex with men or anti-foot fetishist?

RudeBlack: you not collectin check from it but you spread it as if you do...whats the reason? how does that represent your personality?

RudeBlack: no im gay

RudeBlack: but im a believing and God fearing man

RudeBlack: that is why such a thing, report or your status message is extremely offensive to me

RudeBlack: the question is, are you anti-God?

ME: spreading it? i placed it on my status message...that's it. i don't consider that spreading it...i think you overestimate the impact my status message has on the world.

RudeBlack: well you let people on your list to read it...i think thats an impact

ME: I don't understand how believing in and/or fearing God leads one to be offended by the report

RudeBlack: thats because you dont believe the Belief most probably

ME: which Belief?

ME: why are you offended by the thought that Jesus did what you do sexually?

RudeBlack: because Jesus did not act physically and did not sin and believing Gods Word, the act of homosexuality is a sin...but its no use explaining it to you because you dont understand the Belief

ME: Didn't act physically? what does that mean?

ME: didn't eat, sleep, fart, shit, piss???

RudeBlack: look i dont find this conversation any good since to make someone understand the belief and accept it is not a matter of a saturday nite yahoo chat...jesus did not act sexually...

RudeBlack: what i want to say is that when you say your status message represents your personality it means you are against God...

RudeBlack: which i can tolerate...

RudeBlack: but I cant accept the fact you are practically insulting people that believe Jesus was a Holy Man...

RudeBlack: much more offensive than if your status was " black people are murderers" or " gay people are retarted"

ME: how do you know that Jesus didn't act sexually?

RudeBlack: because the Word says so

ME: the Word says he didn't have sex?

RudeBlack: i believe the Word more than yahoo news

RudeBlack: yes!

RudeBlack: Jesus did not come to change the Law given to Moses

RudeBlack: which says that sex before marriage is illegal and he wasnt married

RudeBlack: and the Law also said that homosexuality is a sin

RudeBlack: and Jesus didnt sin

ME: If the law (covenant) wasn't changed then there wouldn't have been a distinction made between the Old Testament and the New Testament.

RudeBlack: you misunderstand...old testament is the word given before Jesus simply...but jesus didnt come to abolish the law but to fulfill it, in new testament

RudeBlack: old testament is a collection of books of many prophets that came before Jesus

RudeBlack: new testament is purely Book of Jesus

RudeBlack: and Quran fulfills the Message

ME: you're muslim?

RudeBlack: yes?

ME: ok

ME: well that explains a lot

RudeBlack: like what

ME: like your belief

RudeBlack: i believe its same offensive for moslim as for a christian

ME: i think that depends on the Muslim or Christian involved

ME: So you believe every time you suck a dick that you are sinning?

RudeBlack: yes i do

ME: that must really contribute to your dick sucking skills.

RudeBlack: fuck off

ME: I would have expected a diligent Muslim to say As Salaam Alaikum...not "fuck off".

ME: but I'll respond with Walaikum As Salaam

RudeBlack: thats for another diligent moslim not someone who says jesus is a faggot

ME: Actually the Salaam's are for the giver of them. It's part of your work as a Muslim not for the benefit of the receiver

ME: get your pillars together Haqqi

RudeBlack: im obliged to say salam only to moslim (the one devoted to Allahs will) and also as reply

RudeBlack: and its not a pillar

ME: and for the record I never said Jesus was a faggot

ME: I said he had sex with men, was a lover of men, and had a foot fetish
ME: that doesn't make him a faggot
ME: any more than it makes you a faggot
ME: so you assumed I'm not a Muslim
ME: and i didn't say it was a pillar...i said you need to get your pillars together
RudeBlack: my pillars are not up to me to get together...and u are not moslim believing that Jesus was homosexual or foofetishist...
ME: Now you're going to determine my connection to Allah?
RudeBlack: i gtg [got to go]...please think twice before setting your status message...
ME: are you Shi'ite?
ME: are you a Ayatollah?
RudeBlack: Im sunni!
ME: you gonna interpret Allah for me?
ME: so than you should know better
ME: it's not your place to interpret Islam for/to me
ME: I am a Sufi Muslim
RudeBlack: im not interpretin islam to u
RudeBlack: thats what u do
ME: Can I ask you a question? How did I get on your buddy list in the first place? Have we spoken before?
ME: You're whole discussion with me has been to tell me what I should believe and how I should believe and how what I believe is wrong
ME: You're tryin to tell me that you have the True Islam and I don't
RudeBlack: if u say u a moslim u shud know what to believe and believing jesus was gay is against islam
ME: You are being divisive in your practice
ME: That is your belief
ME: I believe differently
RudeBlack: islam is one belief
ME: and I'm still waiting for my Salaams
RudeBlack: sorry i cant give you salams since you didnt convince me you are moslim but you convinced me you are nonbeliever
ME: Now I have to convince you that I'm a Believer? You really sound

like a Shi'ite now. You sure you're not down with Osama?

RudeBlack: what are you saying? Osama? he isnt Shi'ite! and im not down with no one but God!

ME: i'm saying you're Shi'ite and down with Osama

ME: based upon your practice

RudeBlack: what practise?

RudeBlack: islam is my practice!

ME: sounds to me like dogma is your practice and your belief

RudeBlack: what are you talking about? what dogma???

ME: sounds like love, beauty, and passion have left your practice and belief

ME: Where's your Peace, brother? Where's the Peace believing that your God-given love for men is a sin?

ME: There is no Al' Islam in your Islam.

ME: and it shows

RudeBlack: its not up to you to judge! and what shows in ur islam? that you are against the islam

ME: How does Paradise show up in your heart if you believe your heart has betrayed you in loving other men?

ME: Oh now you don't like it when judgement turns to what's in your heart as a True Believer, a Follower of the Prophets, a Conformer to the Way of God.

RudeBlack: you cant change islam to what you like!

RudeBlack: islam is islam

RudeBlack: it doesnt change

ME: I don't need to change Islam to what I like because I know that Islam likes me...you don't believe Islam likes you, which is why you hate yourself

ME: That hatred of yourself is against the way of Islam

RudeBlack: islam is not a person to like you!

RudeBlack: i have more love and peace within that you will ever know

ME: you can't believe in the infallibility of Allah as the Creator of ALL THINGS and believe that any part of you should be hated

ME: That my friend is where you are failing as a Muslim...not when you have a dick in your mouth or in your ass.

ME: Until you believe in the total infallibility of Allah as the CREATOR OF ALL THINGS even the desire in your heart for other men, you will always be a dogmatic rather than a TRUE BELIEVER

SPECIAL NOTE: There was no Jesus report nor a Yahoo! article about a Jesus Report.

TO LIVE

To live
with a clear mind
undisturbed by the madness,
    the Sadness, the egoness of
a myth from some folks reality.

Oh, to live
it is the very isness of
    I am
the creative union of a Soular
functioning.

Oh, to live
to be in the irreducible
fashion of existence and feel
     the smooth, soothing rhythms
of a correctness that can not be
dismissed by the heretics of the
conglomerate.

Oh, to live
in the it is I and to
     know that it was never a question
of to be or not to be
but of when to be and
     when to be even more.

Call it the, to live thing
to be thing, to I thing
     but don't call it too late
don't call it when the hum
of the drum is dumb
call it
call it as, during, while
call it before, because, be there

To live
not the impossible dream
but the predestined dream
the unquestionable dream
because being in the, to live
only manifests dreams into reality
and the illusion of nonexistence
lasts only in the minds of
the ignorant, for even
     the dead have the ability
To live.

THE EROTIC AS AFFINITY: HOW I BECAME A GODFATHER AND QUEER DADDY

Erotic: (n) 1. "A measure between the beginnings of our sense of self and the chaos of our strongest feelings." 2. "It is an internal sense of satisfaction to which, once we have experienced it, we know we can aspire. For having experienced the fullness of this depth of feeling and recognizing its power, in honor and self-respect, we can require no less of ourselves." 3. "Those physical, emotional, and psychic expressions of what is deepest and strongest and richest within each of us, being shared: the passion of love, in its deepest meanings."

From Audre Lorde's *Use of the Erotic: The Erotic as Power*

Throughout my twenties and early thirties, I loved fucking twenty-something young men. Young men, aged 23-26, really turned me on. I had a preference for them actually. I liked the boyish faces, the supple, toned bodies, the blemish-free skin, and the way their faces formed an expression of ecstasy when they were getting fucked. It seemed that almost all of them had huge dicks. I loved penetrating a man with a big dick and they seemed to, as an age cohort, disproportionately have them. I began to suspect that their generation had been the first to be exposed to growth hormones in foods, particularly milk, which contributed to physiological changes such as bigger dicks among boys and bigger breasts among girls. Suffice it to say, the sex with them was usually very good, if not great, but my attempts to engage them in ongoing relationships were met with disastrous results.

What usually happened was that while these men could provide what I wanted sexually, they could not provide what I needed *emotionally* and/or *intellectually*. Having had relationships with several very powerful women, I had developed a capacity for and an expectation of a certain level of emotional engagement. I had become accustomed to reflecting upon and discussing my feelings, thoughts, and actions from a deep place of connectedness. I valued opportunities for vulnerability, experiencing and providing emotional support, and intimacy that was not a precursor for sexual activity.

Being a former nerd turned intellectual, I also enjoyed intellectually engaging lovers/partners/fuck buddies. A stimulating discussion of politics, society, spirituality, or culture could go a long way to getting me to erection. The young men who I fucked during that time, with a few exceptions, did not have that kind of intellectual stimulation to give. They hadn't read much, weren't familiar with geopolitical analysis, and didn't have a background in Black Studies. There were serious differences in worldviews and consciousnesses between my sexual mates and me.

These emotional and intellectual incompatibilities and sexual compatibilities produced very difficult relationships and interactions. Intense sexual passion existed alongside barren gulfs of emotional and intellectual engagement. Yet, whenever I locked eyes with another twenty-something, exchanging the intensity of desire, I was ready to fuck, suck, and kiss my way into another problematic interaction. Then something changed—I ended the 10-year relationship I had with a sister, moved out of her place and into my own. That act of simultaneous divorce and self-re-creation created space for me to envision new possibilities for my relationships.

214

Charly

I had seen and interacted with Charly in the community for years. I was very attracted to and aroused by him. He had a soft energy to him that really appealed to me. At the same time, I loved the cultural aesthetic that he expressed in his form of dress. I never got the feeling that he was down to hook up with me. He was warm and polite but he didn't give, "let's fuck," though that was definitely my desire. A friend of his rented my space for an event and Charly came through.

Within minutes of him entering the space, he went into possession. Reacting to the altars/shrines and the energies of the spirits and ancestors that had been living with me at the time, Charly was triggered into a heavy possession by his spirits and ancestors. I immediately started to work with him to acknowledge and communicate with them. All of this while, the event was occurring in another part of my space. Eventually, his consciousness was able to reassert its centrality and we talked. I found him to be very spiritually gifted. Through that experience and the subsequent discussions that occurred immediately afterward, I uncovered the reasons for the attraction that I had experienced for Charly for all that time. My sexual desire was actually a much larger desire, an erotic desire. There was a need that we each had to be engaged with each other on a deep, emotional-spiritual level.

He and I worked on his relationship with his spirit-warriors and ancestors for weeks and in the process developed a bond that we eventually formalized as a godfather-godson relationship. As Charly's godfather, I have committed to working with him to nurture his healthy development as human being. I counsel him on matters of spirit, the heart, and everyday life issues. It is a very intimate relationship, physically, emotionally, and spiritually. We do not have sex or sexual contact but there is sexual kinetic energy that travels between us. We don't need to be each other's lover. But we are in love with each other. We experience each other in such rich and meaningful ways.

The relationship didn't just become what it is overnight. It evolved over time as we both learned about it, which was a new form of relationship for both of us, as we built it together. I don't mean to convey that the godparent relationship was new to either one of us, because it wasn't. But neither of us had experienced or were exposed to such a relationship that not only acknowledged the presence of sexual attraction but also found a way to position that sexual attraction in a way that was healthy and liberating for all of those involved. We learned not to run from or deny the sexual energy that travels between us or to fall into it by fucking.

Though there is much that I am responsible for providing Charly as his godfather, I have gotten much from the relationship. I have learned the power of the erotic to create affinities between folks that can foster powerful connections. I became liberated through the relationship, no longer being held to the belief that my erotic desire for a person demanded fulfillment in sexual contact. I was opened to other possibilities for relating to someone to whom I felt a profound attraction. In my mid-thirties, I found a more fulfilling, productive way of being in relationship to and interacting with twenty-somethings, as a mentor rather than sexual experience.

Pharon

I had also seen Pharon around New York City, at different events in the community. We saw each other online, communicating through our profiles on the sex web site of which we were both members. Unlike Charly's energy, Pharon did convey that he wanted to fuck. In a number of our chance meetings, we flirted and let it be known to each other that we thought the other was hot and we wanted to fuck. We exchanged numbers. Talked on the phone a few times. But we never could seem to orchestrate a date to hook up and fuck. Then came Our Bodies, Our Wisdom (OBOW).

The creation of OBOW was the focus of my doctoral dissertation. OBOW is a collaborative inquiry, human development, encounter group process that incorporates Sensual Yoga, Theatre of the Oppressed, and African ritual as methods. I originally developed it working with a group of six men of African-descent who experienced same-sex desire. After the successful implementation of the process for my dissertation research, I decided to continue to offer it to folks (i.e., men, women, trans, etc.) in a modified form. Pharon heard about one of the offerings and registered for one of the OBOW retreats.

When he registered for the retreat, I thought to myself, "This is going to be interesting." By that time, both he and I were in relationships. His was polyamorous; mine was monogamous. Our partners were going to be at the retreat. In addition to those dynamics, the nature of OBOW would, I knew, also add some spice to the mix. OBOW is a very intimate, intense experience for participants and facilitators. There are long periods of physical and/or emotional nudity. That, in and of itself, creates intensity. Imagine practicing yoga in the nude and performing certain *asanas* with a partner or group of partners. And that's just an example of the physical nudity.

Pharon came to the retreat and impressed me with his depth of spirit, his insight, and his ability to be self-reflective. As I do with each participant after OBOW, I spoke with him after the experience to debrief and process his experience. He shared with me how profound it was for him and his desire to continue to be in touch with me in an ongoing way to make additional progress in those areas of his life highlighted during the retreat. Our discussions eventually led to our godfather-godson relationship.

We have a deeply erotic relationship. From an outsider's perspective, our interaction might be mistaken for lovers given the intensity of our exchange, particularly when we are talking or hanging out. But that is not what we have been called to be in each other's lives. The intimacy, love, and affection that we share are parts of a primordial tradition that feeds both of us. We could, if we chose to, fuck each other at any moment, yet that wouldn't bring us any closer together or make the experience of each other any more passionate. Though it is a challenge at times not to do that, I am clear about what would be lost for us in doing so. Because of the power of the sexual scripts we internalize over the years about relating to others, we would lose the flexibility, ingenuity, and creativity in our actions that are so important in a mentorship relationship.

Darius

Darius and I met online while he was living here in NY. We met specifically to fuck. Darius and I had kink in common. He liked to sub and I liked to Dom. Darius has a loving disposition with a piercing curiosity. When you had information that he wanted, Darius could dig the shit out of a topic of conversation. At the same time, you can see the tinge of sadness that sits in his eyes.

Through our sex and the conversations that were interspersed between the sex, I could tell Darius needed, wanted, and could benefit from a mentor, a father figure, in his life. I became Darius' Queer Daddy and he became my son. I coined the term Queer Daddy, borrowing from the term *Daddy* in the Bondage Domination/Submission Sadomasochism (BDSM) and Leather-Kink communities, to describe a dominant relational role that includes aspects of the BDSM, Leather-Kink Daddy as well as the characteristics of mentorship and eldership that are a part of non-sexual community conceptualizations of mentors.

Darius was my first son and our relationship predated my relationships with Charly and Pharon. My relationship with him helped frame the possibility of creating a Queer family. It demonstrated to me what could be gained by forming tribes, families, or houses of affinity as queer people. We were building a counter-culture in our validation of the erotic, a counter-culture that was intimate, personal, and earthy. As a result of these experiences, queer family development has been a major part of my social justice organizing.

Unlike my relationships with Charly and Pharon, Darius and I have had sex. In fact, part of how Darius demonstrates his appreciation for my role in his life as a mentor, counselor, and adviser is to perform sexual acts merely for my fulfillment and pleasure. Very much like the bonding and initiatory practices of Indigenous men and young men of the Pacific, part of the way I transmit my energy as a man is through the ritualized sexual practices that Darius and I perform. The sex is deeply personal and intimate. Many of the sexual acts in which we engage are quite different from the sex that men usually perform with each other. Because those acts are part of a ritualistic process, I will not share details. They are parts of sacred, secret knowledge. To reveal them would be to diminish them of their psychic and ritualistic energy.

Our relationship has survived the various lovers I have had, the many cities in which we have both lived, and the busyness of our schedules. We have made time for each other through it all. I gave him feedback on his graduate school personal essays, counseled him while he managed a complicated relationship with a friend, and provided him with contacts before he went overseas for work.

Junior

Junior and I met online also. We lived in different states. Spirit would eventually put us in a position to meet offline. I attended a conference in his city and we planned to meet. I was in a monogamous relationship at the time and had decided to manage the meeting so that I would not be overcome by any sexual tension between the two of us. When we finally met, Junior's boyish curiosity, playfulness, and shyness were clearly evident. In his early twenties at the time, Junior clearly looked up to me and I could feel his desire to be looking up to me in bed as well. He was very cute with a slight Caribbean accent that I enjoyed.

We hung out that night, eating, talking, and driving around his city. It was fun and just a little tense given that I wanted to fuck him, he wanted me to fuck him, and I was committed to the monogamy of the relationship I had. We ended the night—without incident—and continued talking online as we had before, but now with the experience of having been in each other's physical presence to inform our online interactions.

I began counseling him as he dealt with difficulties in a relationship he started with another older man. When that relationship ended and he started dating other men, I gave him advice. We had deep conversations about life, love, and the world. The erotic potential between the two of us developed through those conversations. Eventually, we acknowledged the love that had grown between us. I shared with Junior the concept of a Daddy/son relationship. He was intrigued. He appreciated having a way to define/describe what had emerged. Junior became my youngest son—the baby, as he likes to describe himself in relation to Darius, Pharon, and Charly.

Because he and I have shared the least amount of time together physically (as compared with Charly and Pharon) and he hasn't gotten to have sex with his Daddy (as compared to Darius), he is, sometimes, jealous of the other members of our queer family but for the most part it is a playful sibling rivalry. Junior is an important member of my queer family despite the distance and infrequency of face-to-face contact. My relationship with him affirms for me the power of the erotic to transcend physical proximity when the affinity is so strong.

We still hold out the possibility of having sex or being sexual. Junior fetishizes my body type and the age difference between us (as do I). I get off on his youthfulness and the way he uses it to flirt and make himself sexually available. Those things make the possibility of sex a question of when rather than if. As long as our relationship statuses don't preclude our fucking, Daddy and son will make it happen, one day.

All four of these relationships have been deeply meaningful to me. The relationships and the men who have been a part of them have taught me so much about my capacity to love, to express the erotic, and to be in tune with how I share affinity with others. I cherish what I have gained and who I have become as a result of my connections to Junior, Darius, Pharon, and Charly. Thank you, my sons and godsons.

THE OATH OF
SEXUAL-SPIRITUAL
LIBERATION AND CULTIVATION

I proclaim the power and purpose of my sexual journey. I am committed to learning from each erotic experience and each sensual moment without diminishing the meaning of the sheer joy and pleasure such experiences offer.

I declare myself a member of many communities of being and cherish the connectedness I share with others. I endeavor to honor that connectedness in each touch, caress, lick, suck, fuck, orgasm, bite, swallow, in every act of passion, lust, or desire I share.

I renounce any barrier, limitation, or expectation placed upon my relationship with the sexual core of this earth and universe. I disavow any authority of those who seek to exploit my erotic power in their own parasitic interests.

I invoke the spirits of play, creativity, joy, passion, curiosity, humility, and vigilance as my companions and counselors along this sexual journey of mine. I offer myself, with all my frailties and fortitudes, as a vehicle for self-discovery and self-mastery for others as they make their sexual journey.

Finally, I affirm my commitment to not take myself too seriously as I grow, learn, and stumble along the journey.

Ache, amen.

Bibliography

Akbar, N., Saafir, R., & Granberry, D. (1996). Community psychology and systems intervention. In D. A. Azibo (Ed.), *African Psychology in Historical Perspective and Related Commentary* (pp. 149-184). Trenton, NJ: Africa World Press.

Alexander, M. J. (2005). *Pedagogies of crossing: Meditations on Feminism, sexual politics, memory, and the Sacred.* Durham, NC: Duke University Press.

Altman, D. (2001). Rupture or continuity? The internationalization of gay identity. In J.C. Hawley (Ed.), *Post-Colonial Queer: Theoretical Intersections* (pp. 19-42). New York: State University of New York Press.

Ani, M. (1994). *Yurugu: An African-centered critique of European cultural thought and behavior.* Trenton, NJ: Africa World Press.

Anzaldua, G. (1999). *Borderlands: La frontera—the new mestiza, 2nd edition.* San Francisco: Aunt Lute Books.

Asante, M. (1987). *Afrocentric idea.* Philadelphia: Temple University Press.

Asante, M. (1988). *Afrocentricity.* Trenton, NJ: African World Press.

Ashby, M. (2005). *Sacred sexuality: Ancient Egyptian tantric yoga.* FL: Sema Institute.

Azibo, D. A. (1996). Mental health defined Africentrically. In D. A. ya Azibo (Ed.), *African Psychology in Historical Perspective and Related Commentary* (pp. 47-56). Trenton, NJ: Africa World Press.

Beam, J. (1986). Brother to brother: words from the heart. In J. Beam (Ed.), *In the life: A Black Gay Anthology* (pp. 230-242). Boston: Alyson Publications.

Bedfellows, D. (1996). *Policing public sex: Queer politics and the future of AIDS activism.* Cambridge, MA: South End Press.

Bennett, L. (1982). *Before the Mayflower: A history of Black America, 5th ed.* New York: Penguin Books.

Bleys, R. (1995). *The geography of perversion: Male-to-Male sexual behavior outside the West and the ethnographic imagination, 1750-1918.* New York: New York University Press.

Boal, A. (1979). *Theatre of the oppressed.* New York: Theatre Communications.

Boal, A. (1992). *Games for actors and non-actors.* New York: Routledge.

Boal. A. (1995). *The rainbow of desire: The Boal method of theatre and therapy.* New York: Routledge.

Boal, A. (1998). *Legislative theatre: Using performance to make politics.* New York: Routledge.

Boykin, K. (2003). Black gay men and AIDS. Retrieved May 25, 2005, from *http://www.keithboykin.com/arch/000600.html*

Butler, J. (1999). *Gender trouble: Feminism and the subversion of identity.* New York: Routledge.

Butler, O. (1995). *Parable of the sower.* New York: Warner Books/Aspect.

Butler, O. (1999). *Wild seed.* New York: Warner Books/Aspect.

Bynum, E. (1999). *The African unconscious: Roots of ancient mysticism and modern psychology.* New York: Teachers College Press.

Califia, P. (1994). *Public sex: The culture of radical sex.* San Francisco: Cleis Press.

Carruthers, J. (1999). *Intellectual warfare*. Chicago: Third World Press.

Centers for Disease Control (2001). t of HIV prevention interventions with evidence of effectiveness. Retrieved May 25, 2005, from *http://www.cdc.gov/hiv/pubs/hivcompendium/ HIVcompendium.htm*

Christian, B. (1990). The race for theory. In G. Anzaldua (Ed.), *Making Face, Making Soul: Hacienda Caras* (pp.334-345). San Francisco: aunt lute books.

Cohen, C. J. (1997). *Punks, bulldaggers, and welfare queens: The radical potential of queer politics*. GLQ, 3(4): 437-465.

Collins, P. H. (2004). *Black sexual politics: African Americans, gender, and the new racism*. New York: Routledge.

Conners, R. P. & Sparks, D. H. (2004). *Queering Creole spiritual traditions: Lesbian, gay, bisexual, and transgender participation in African inspired traditions in the Americas*. Binghamton, NY: Harrington Park Press.

Critical Resistance (2005). Not so common language. Retrieved June 19, 2005, from *http://www.criticalresistance.org/article.php?id=49*

Davis, A. (1981). *Women, race, and class*. New York: Random House.

Davis, K. & Farajaje-Jones, E. (1991). *African creative expressions of the Divine*. Washington, D. C.: Howard University School of Divinity.

Delany, S. R. (2001). *Times Square red, Times Square blue*. New York: New York University Press.

Delany, S. R. (2002). *The mad man*. Rutherford, NJ: Voyant Publishing.

Delany, S. R. (2004a). *Hogg*. Tallahassee, FL: Fiction Collective 2.

Delany, S. R. (2004b). *The motion of light in water: Sex and science fiction writing in the East Village.* Minneapolis, MN: University of Minneapolis Press.

Diop, C. (1974). *The African origin of civilization.* Brooklyn, NY: Lawrence Hill Books.

Diop, C. (1991). *Civilization or barbarism: An authentic anthropology.* Chicago: Lawrence Hill Books.

Douglas, N. & Slinger, P. (1999). *Sexual secrets, twentieth anniversary edition: The alchemy of ecstasy.* Rochester, VT: Destiny Books.

Duran, E. & Duran, B. (1995). *Native American postcolonial psychology.* Albany: State University of New York Press.

Eisler, R. (1988). *The chalice and the blade: Our history, our future.* San Francisco: Harper and Row.

Eisler, R. (1995). *Sacred pleasure: Sex, myth, and the politics of the body–new paths to power and love.* New York: Harper Collins Publishers.

Fanon, F. (1963). *The wretched of the earth.* New York: Grove Press.

Fanon, F. (1965). *A dying colonialism.* New York: Grove Press.

Fanon, F. (1967). *Toward the African revolution.* New York: Grove Press.

Farajaje-Jones, E. (1993). Breaking Silence: Toward an in-the-life theology. In J. Cone & G. Wilmore (Eds.), *Black Theology: A Documentary History* (Volume 2), 1980-1992 (pp.139-159). Maryknoll, NY: Orbis Books.

Farajaje-Jones, E. (2000). Holy fuck. In K. Kay, J. Nagle, & B. Gould (Eds.), *Male Lust: Pleasure, Power, and Transformation* (pp. 327-335). New York: Harrington Park Press.

Farrow, K. (2006). The Voodoo that we do: Discovering my sexual/political/spiritual Self. In G. W. James & L. C. Moore (Eds.), *Spirited: Affirming The Soul And Black Gay/Lesbian Identity* (pp.111-121). Washington, DC: Red Bone Press.

Fausto-Sterling, A. (2000). *Sexing the body: Gender politics and the construction of sexuality.* New York: Basic Books.

Foucault, M. (1988). *Madness and civilization: A history of insanity in the age of reason.* New York: Vintage Books.

Foucault, M. (1990). *The history of sexuality: An introduction, volume 1.* New York: Vintage Books.

Foucault, M. (1995). *Discipline and punish: The birth of the prison.* New York: Vintage Books.

Foucault, M. (1997). *Society must be defended: Lectures at the Collège de France, 1975-1976.* New York: Picador.

Freire, P. (1996). *Pedagogy of hope: Reliving pedagogy of the oppressed.* New York: Continuum.

Freire, P. (1997). *Education for critical consciousness.* New York: Continuum.

Griaule, M. & Dieterlen, G. (1986). *The pale fox.* Chino Valley, Arizona: Continuum Foundation.

Hawley, J. C. (2001). Introduction. In J. C. Hawley (Ed.), *Post-Colonial Queer: Theoretical Intersections* (pp. 1-18). New York: State University of New York Press.

Hemphill, E. (1991). *Brother to brother: Collected writings by Black gay men.* New York: Alyson Books.

Hemphill, E. (2000). *Ceremonies: Prose and poetry.* New York. Plume.

Hillard, A. (1998). *Sba: The reawakening of the African mind*. Atlanta, GA: Makare Publishing.

Hoff, B. (1993). Gays: guardians at the gates—an interview with Malidoma Somé. Retrieved January 5, 2003, from *http://www.menweb.org/somegay.htm*.

hooks, b. (1994). *Teaching to transgress: Education as the practice of freedom*. New York: Routledge.

Humphreys, L. (1975). *Tearoom trade: Impersonal sex in public places*. Edison, NJ: Aldine Transaction.

Jackson, J. (2000). *Man, God, and civilization*. Chicago: Lushena Books.

James, L. (2003). The implications of connections. HIVPlus Retrieved on May 25, 2005, from *http://hivplusmag.com/column.asp?id=21&categoryid=3*

Jochanan, Y. (1988). *Africa: Mother of Western civilization*. New York: Black Classic Press.

Johnson, E. P. (1998). Feeling the spirit in the dark: Expanding notions of the sacred in the African American gay community. *Callaloo*, 21(1): 399-416.

Kambon, K. (1996). The Africentric paradigm and African-American psychological liberation. In D. A. ya Azibo (Ed.), *African Psychology in Historical Perspective and Related Commentary* (pp.57-70). Trenton, NJ: Africa World Press.

Kaphagawani, D. & Malherbe, J. (2002). African epistemology. In P.H. Coetzee & A.P.J. Roux (Eds.), *The African Philosophy Reader, 2nd Edition*. (pp.219-229). London: Routledge.

King, J. (2004). *On the down low: A journey into the lives of "straight" Black men who sleep with men*. New York: Broadway.

Kunnie, J. E. & Goduka, N. I. (2006). *Indigenous peoples' wisdom and power: Affirming our knowledge through narratives*. Aldershot, Hampshire: Ashgate Publishing.

Life, M. (2003). *Spiritual polyamory*. Lincoln, NE: iUniverse.

Lorde, A. (1992). Use of the erotic: The erotic as power. In M. Decosta-Willis, R. Martin, & R. P. Bell (Eds.), *Erotique Noire: Black Erotica* (pp. 78-83). New York: Anchor Books.

Matory, J. L. (1994). *Sex and the empire that is no more: Gender and the politics of metaphor in Oyo Yoruba religion*. Minneapolis, MN: University of Minnesota Press.

Mbiti, J. (1992). *African religions and philosophies, 2nd edition*. Portsmouth, NH: Heinemann.

Mercer, K. (1994). *Welcome to the jungle: New positions in Black cultural studies*. London: Routledge.

Memmi, A. (1965). *The colonizer and the colonized*. Boston: Beacon Press.

Midori. (2002). *The seductive art of Japanese bondage*. Emeryville, CA: Greenery Press.

Mohanty, C. T. (2003). *Feminism without borders: Decolonizing theory, practicing solidarity*. Durham: Duke University Press.

Moraga, C. & Anzaldua, G. (2002). *This bridge called my back: Writings by radical women of color*. Berkeley, CA: Third Woman Press.

Muñoz, J. E. (1999). *Disidentifications: Queers of color and the performance of politics*. Minneapolis: University of Minnesota Press.

Murray, S. O., & Roscoe, W. (1998). *Boy-wives and female husbands: Studies in African homosexualities*. New York: Palgrave.

Myers, L. (1993). *Understanding an Afrocentric worldview: Introduction to an optimal psychology (2nd ed.).* Dubuque, IA: Kendall/Hunt Publishing.

Neumann, E. (1963). *The great mother: An analysis of the archetype, 2nd edition.* Princeton, NJ: Princeton University Press.

Newton, H. P. (2002c). Intercommunalism: February 1971. In D. Hilliard & D. Weise (Eds.), *The Huey P. Newton Reader* (pp.181-199). New York: Seven Stories Press.

Nkrumah, K. (1970). *Consciencism: Philosophy and ideology for decolonization.* New York: Monthly Review Press.

Palmer, B. (2000). *Culture of darkness: Night travels in the histories of transgression–From medieval to modern.* New York: Monthly Review Press.

Ramose, M. (2002). The philosophy of ubuntu and ubuntu as a philosophy. In P.H. Coetzee & A.P.J. Roux (Eds.), *The African Philosophy Reader, 2nd Edition.* (pp.230-238). London: Routledge.

Reed, I. (1996). *Mumbo jumbo.* New York: Scribner.

Research, Development, and Statistics Directorate of Home Office (2003). World prison population list, 5th edition. Retrieved June 15, 2005, from *http://www.homeoffice.gov.uk/rds/pdfs2/r234.pdf*

Rodney, W. (1981). *How Europe underdeveloped Africa.* Washington DC: Howard University Press.

Rofes, E. (1996). *Reviving the tribe: Regenerating gay men's sexuality and culture in the ongoing epidemic.* Binghamton, NY: Haworth Press.

Rofes, E. (1998). *Dry bones breathe: Gay men creating post-AIDS identities and cultures.* Binghamton, NY: Haworth Press.

Sandoval, C. (2000). *Methodology of the oppressed.* Minnesota: University of Minnesota Press.

Saint, A. (1996). *Spells of a Voodoo doll: The poems, fiction, essays, and plays of Assotto Saint.* New York: Richard Kasak Books.

Santiago, S. (2002). The wily homosexual (First—and necessarily hasty—notes). In A. Cruz-Malavé & M. F. Manalansan IV (Eds.), *Queer Globalizations: Citizenship and the Afterlife of Colonialism* (pp.13-19). New York: New York University Press.

Shlain, L. (1998). *The alphabet versus the Goddess: The conflict between word and image.* New York: Compass/Penguin.

Shlain, L. (2004). *Sex, time, and power: How women's sexuality shaped human evolution.* New York: Penguin.

Sigal, P. (2000). *From moon goddesses to virgins: The colonization of Yucatecan Mayan sexual desire.* Austin, TX: University of Texas Press.

Simmons, R. (1991). Some thoughts on the challenges facing Black gay intellectuals. In E. Hemphill (Ed.), *Brother to Brother: Collected Writings by Black Gay Men* (pp.211-228). New York: Alyson Books.

Sjöö, M. & Mor, B. (1987) *The great cosmic mother: Discovering the religion of the earth.* New York: HarperCollins Publishers.

Somé, M. (1998). *The healing wisdom of Africa: Finding life purpose through nature, ritual, and community.* New York: Jeremy P. Tarcher/Putnam.

Somé, M. (2004). *The gift of the gatekeepers.* Unpublished manuscript. Chico, CA.

Somé, S. (2003). Homosexuality: The gatekeepers. Retrieved July 6, 2003, from *http://w3.ime.net/~bmbc/soulvpo3.htm.*

Sparrowe, L. (2005). The history of yoga. Retrieved May 8, 2005, from *http://www.yogajournal.com/history/.*

Stoler, A. (1995). *Race and the education of desire: Foucault's history of sexuality and the colonial order of things.* Durham, NC: Duke University Press.

Taussig, M. (1987). *Shamanism, colonialism, and the wild man: A study in terror and healing.* Chicago: University of Chicago Press.

Teffo, L. J. & Roux, A. P. J. (2002). Themes in African metaphysics. In P. H. Coetzee & A. P. J. Roux (Eds.), *The African Philosophy Reader, 2nd Edition* (pp. 161-174). New York: Routledge.

Teish, L. (1988). *Jambalaya: The natural woman's book of personal charms and practical rituals.* San Francisco: HarperSanFrancisco.

T'Shaka, O. (1995). *Return to the African mother principle of male and female equality, volume one.* Oakland, CA: Pan Afrikan Publishers and Distributors.

Vishnu-devananda, S. (1988). *The complete illustrated book of yoga.* New York: Harmony Books.

Washington, H. (2007). *Medical apartheid: The dark history of medical experimentation on Black Americans from colonial times to the present.* New York: Doubleday.

White, E. F. (2001). *Dark continents of our bodies: Black feminism and the politics of respectability.* Philadelphia: Temple University Press.

Williams, C. (1987). *The destruction of Black civilization: Great issues of a race from 4500 BC to 2000 AD.* Chicago: Third World Press.

Williams, E. (1984). *From Columbus to Castro: The history of the Caribbean, 1492-1969.* New York: Vintage Books.

Williams, H. S. (2006). Our bodies, our wisdom: Engaging Black men who experience same-sex desire in Afrocentric ritual, embodied epistemology, and collaborative inquiry. *Dissertation Abstracts International, 67*(02), 618A. (UMI No. 3208854)

Williams, H. S, (2006, December 5). Decolonizing and reconstructing epistemologies, methodologies, and practices?. From the Cave. Retrieved January 31, 2007, from *http://www.blackfunk.org/funk/ modules.php?name=News&file=article&sid=115&mode=&order=0&thold=0*

Williams, W. (1992). *Spirit and the flesh: Sexual diversity in American Indian culture.* Boston: Beacon Press.

Young, R. (1995). *Colonial desire: Hybridity in theory, culture, and race.* New York: Routledge.

About the Author

Aih Djehuti Herukhuti Khepera Ra Temu Seti Amen is a sociologist/anthropologist, sexologist, educator, shaman, BDSM practitioner, artist, cultural animator, and author. He is the founder of Black Funk, a sexual cultural center dedicated to providing a space for the exhibition and exploration of sensual awareness, sexual consciousness, erotic power, and pleasure. Black Funk is a gathering place for sexually liberated people of color to express themselves and enjoy erotic events, demonstrations, and sexuality-related classes. Since 1998, Black Funk has reached thousands of people around the world with its programs and services including Erotic Fight Club, Sensual Yoga, and its relationship and sexuality coaching services. In 2004, Black Funk launched the popular, raw web site blackfunk.org, providing users with an online source for news, information, and community on topics related to culture, sexuality, and spirituality from a conscious, funky perspective.

A Dom/Daddy with two sons and two godsons, Herukhuti is the head of a vibrant, passionate, and committed BDSM queer family that combines traditional African values in a contemporary BDSM/queer context. He provides training and education for those interested in Afrocentric, BDSM/queer lifestyles and family configurations.

Herukhuti has contributed to the development of the perspective known as Afrocentric, Decolonizing Queer Theory, a way of understanding how Blackness and queerness are culturally, spiritually, and sexually interconnected as sources of liberatory power. He is the architect of the human development group process, Our Bodies, Our Wisdom, which incorporates yoga, Theatre of the Oppressed, and African ritual to assist people in collaborative problem-solving and critical reflection.
Drawing from the knowledge he has gained from his unique background, Herukhuti is a compelling speaker, workshop/retreat facilitator, and author. His plays have been produced at the New York International Fringe Theatre Festival. His writing has appeared in *Arise Magazine. Ma-Ka: Diasporic Juks—Contemporary Writings by Queers of African Descent, African Voices, Women In The Life: The Premier Lesbian Website and Monthly,* and *Think Again* as well as in various academic journals and publications.

Herukhuti holds degrees in psychology and political science from the University of Southern California, an MEd in curriculum and instruction from Lesley University, and a PhD in human and organizational systems from Fielding Graduate University where he earned a concentration in transformative learning for social justice and specialized in sexuality and cross-cultural studies of knowledge systems. Initiated into the Shrine of Amen Ra at the age of 14 by Khafra Ndongo Amen, Herukhuti is a Kemetic priest who has also studied mysticism with the late Sufi master Genghis Nor and Dagara shamanism and cosmology with Dr. Malidoma Somè.

He is on the faculty of the Individualized Study BA Program at Goddard College in Plainfield, Vermont.

You can contact Dr. Herukhuti for consultations at:
Black Funk: The Center for Culture, Sexuality, and Spirituality
http://www.blackfunk.org
info@blackfunk.org
917.403.0536